MY ASIAN WAY 2022

DELICIOUS ASIAN RECIPES TO SURPRISE YOUR GUESTS

EVA CHANG

Table of Contents

Spicy Braised Pork

Serves 4

450 g/1 lb pork, diced

salt and pepper

30 ml/2 tbsp soy sauce

30 ml/2 tbsp hoisin sauce

45 ml/3 tbsp groundnut (peanut) oil

120 ml/4 fl oz/½ cup rice wine or dry sherry

300 ml/½ pt/1¼ cups chicken stock

5 ml/1 tsp five-spice powder

6 spring onions (scallions), chopped

225 g/8 oz oyster mushrooms, sliced

15 ml/1 tbsp cornflour (cornstarch)

Season the meat with salt and pepper. Place in a dish and mix in the soy sauce and hoisin sauce. Cover and leave to marinate for 1 hour. Heat the oil and stir-fry the meat until golden brown. Add the wine or sherry, stock and five-spice powder, bring to the boil, cover and simmer for 1 hour. Add the spring onions and mushrooms, remove the lid and simmer for a further 4 minutes. Blend the cornflour with a little water, bring back to the boil and simmer, stirring, for 3 minutes until the sauce thickens.

Makes 12

30 ml/2 tbsp hoisin sauce

15 ml/1 tbsp oyster sauce

15 ml/1 tbsp soy sauce

2.5 ml/½ tsp sesame oil

30 ml/2 tbsp groundnut (peanut) oil

10 ml/2 tsp grated ginger root

1 clove garlic, crushed

300 ml/½ pt/1¼ cups water

15 ml/1 tbsp cornflour (cornstarch)

225 g/8 oz cooked pork, finely chopped

4 spring onions (scallions), finely chopped

350 g/12 oz/3 cups plain (all-purpose) flour

15 ml/1 tbsp baking powder

2.5 ml/½ tsp salt

50 g/2 oz/½ cup lard

5 ml/1 tsp wine vinegar

12 x 13 cm/5 in greaseproof paper squares

Mix together the hoisin, oyster and soy sauces and the sesame oil. Heat the oil and fry the ginger and garlic until lightly browned. Add the sauce mixture and fry for 2 minutes. Blend

120 ml/4 fl oz/½ cup of the water with the cornflour and stir it into the pan. Bring to the boil, stirring, then simmer until the mixture thickens. Stir in the pork and onions then leave to cool.

Mix together the flour, baking powder and salt. Rub in the lard until the mixture resembles fine breadcrumbs. Mix the wine vinegar and remaining water then mix this into the flour to form a firm dough. Knead lightly on a floured surface then cover and leave to stand for 20 minutes.

Knead the dough again then divide it into 12 and shape each one into a ball. Roll out to 15 cm/6 in circles on a floured surface. Place spoonfuls of the filling in the centre of each circle, brush the edges with water and pinch the edges together to seal around the filling. Brush one side of each greaseproof paper square with oil. Place each bun on a square of paper, seam side down. Place the buns in a single layer on a steamer rack over boiling water. Cover and steam the buns for about 20 minutes until cooked.

Pork with Cabbage

Serves 4

6 dried Chinese mushrooms

30 ml/2 tbsp groundnut (peanut) oil

450 g/1 lb pork, cut into strips

2 onions, sliced

2 red peppers, cut into strips

350 g/12 oz white cabbage, shredded

2 cloves garlic, chopped

2 pieces stem ginger, chopped

30 ml/2 tbsp honey

45 ml/3 tbsp soy sauce

120 ml/4 fl oz/½ cup dry white wine

salt and pepper

10 ml/2 tsp cornflour (cornstarch)

15 ml/1 tbsp water

Soak the mushrooms in warm water for 30 minutes then drain. Discard the stalks and slice the caps. Heat the oil and fry the pork until lightly browned. Add the vegetables, garlic and ginger and stir-fry for 1 minute. Add the honey, soy sauce and wine, bring to the boil, cover and simmer for 40 minutes until the meat is cooked. Season with salt and pepper. Mix together the cornflour and water and stir it into the pan. Bring just up to the boil, stirring continuously, then simmer for 1 minute.

Pork with Cabbage and Tomatoes

Serves 4

30 ml/2 tbsp groundnut (peanut) oil

450 g/1 lb lean pork, cut into slivers

salt and freshly ground pepper

1 clove garlic, crushed

1 onion, finely chopped

½ cabbage, shredded

450 g/1 lb tomatoes, skinned and quartered

250 ml/8 fl oz/1 cup stock

30 ml/2 tbsp cornflour (cornstarch)

15 ml/1 tbsp soy sauce

60 ml/4 tbsp water

Heat the oil and fry the pork, salt, pepper, garlic and onion until lightly browned. Add the cabbage, tomatoes and stock, bring to the boil, cover and simmer for 10 minutes until the cabbage is just tender. Blend the cornflour, soy sauce and water to a paste, stir into the pan and simmer, stirring, until the sauce clears and thickens.

Serves 4

350 g/12 oz belly pork

2 spring onions (scallions), chopped

1 slice ginger root, minced

1 stick cinnamon

3 cloves star anise

45 ml/3 tbsp brown sugar

600 ml/1 pt/2½ cups water

15 ml/1 tbsp groundnut (peanut) oil

15 ml/1 tbsp soy sauce

5 ml/1 tsp tomato purée (paste)

5 ml/1 tsp oyster sauce

100 g/4 oz Chinese cabbage hearts

100 g/4 oz pak choi

Cut the pork into 10 cm/4 in chunks and place in a bowl. Add the spring onions, ginger, cinnamon, star anise, sugar and water and leave to stand for 40 minutes. Heat the oil, lift the pork from the marinade and add it to the pan. Fry until lightly browned then add the soy sauce, tomato purée and oyster sauce. Bring to the boil and simmer for about 30 minutes until the pork is tender and the liquid has reduced, adding a little more water during cooking, if necessary.

Meanwhile, steam the cabbage hearts and pak choi over boiling water for about 10 minutes until tender. Arrange them on a warmed serving plate, top with the pork and spoon over the sauce.

Pork with Celery

Serves 4

45 ml/3 tbsp groundnut (peanut) oil

1 clove garlic, crushed

1 spring onion (scallion), chopped

1 slice ginger root, minced

225 g/8 oz lean pork, cut into strips

100 g/4 oz celery, thinly sliced

45 ml/3 tbsp soy sauce

15 ml/1 tbsp rice wine or dry sherry

5 ml/1 tsp cornflour (cornstarch)

Heat the oil and fry the garlic, spring onion and ginger until lightly browned. Add the pork and stir-fry for 10 minutes until golden brown. Add the celery and stir-fry for 3 minutes. Add the remaining ingredients and stir-fry for 3 minutes.

Pork with Chestnuts and Mushrooms

Serves 4

4 dried Chinese mushrooms
100 g/4 oz/1 cup chestnuts
30 ml/2 tbsp groundnut (peanut) oil
2.5 ml/½ tsp salt
450 g/1 lb lean pork, cubed
15 ml/1 tbsp soy sauce
375 ml/13 fl oz/1½ cups chicken stock
100 g/4 oz water chestnuts, sliced

Soak the mushrooms in warm water for 30 minutes then drain. Discard the stalks and halve the caps. Blanch the chestnuts in boiling water for 1 minute then drain. Heat the oil and salt then fry the pork until lightly browned. Add the soy sauce and stir-fry for 1 minute. Add the stock and bring to the boil. Add the chestnuts and water chestnuts, bring back to the boil, cover and simmer for about 1½ hours until the meat is tender.

Pork Chop Suey

Serves 4

100 g/4 oz bamboo shoots, cut into strips

100 g/4 oz water chestnuts, thinly sliced

60 ml/4 tbsp groundnut (peanut) oil

3 spring onions (scallions), chopped

2 cloves garlic, crushed

1 slice ginger root, chopped

225 g/8 oz lean pork, cut into strips

45 ml/3 tbsp soy sauce

15 ml/1 tbsp rice wine or dry sherry

5 ml/1 tsp salt

5 ml/1 tsp sugar

freshly ground pepper

15 ml/1 tbsp cornflour (cornstarch)

Blanch the bamboo shoots and water chestnuts in boiling water for 2 minutes then drain and pat dry. Heat 45 ml/3 tbsp of oil and fry the spring onions, garlic and ginger until lightly browned. Add the pork and stir-fry for 4 minutes. Remove from the pan.

Heat the remaining oil and stir-fry the vegetables for 3 minutes. Add the pork, soy sauce, wine or sherry, salt, sugar and a pinch of pepper and stir-fry for 4 minutes. Mix the cornflour with a little water, stir it into the pan and simmer, stirring, until the sauce clears and thickens.

Pork Chow Mein

Serves 4

4 dried Chinese mushrooms
30 ml/2 tbsp groundnut (peanut) oil
2.5 ml/½ tsp salt
4 spring onions (scallions), chopped
225 g/8 oz lean pork, cut into strips
15 ml/1 tbsp soy sauce
5 ml/1 tsp sugar
3 stalks celery, chopped
1 onion, cut into wedges
100 g/4 oz mushrooms, halved
120 ml/4 fl oz/½ cup chicken stock
soft-fried noodles

Soak the mushrooms in warm water for 30 minutes then drain. Discard the stalks and slice the caps. Heat the oil and salt and fry the spring onions until softened. Add the pork and fry until lightly browned. Mix in the soy sauce, sugar, celery, onion and both fresh and dried mushrooms and stir-fry for about 4 minutes until the ingredients are well blended. Add the stock and simmer for 3 minutes. Add half the noodles to the pan and stir gently, then add the remaining noodles and stir until heated through.

Roast Pork Chow Mein

Serves 4

100 g/4 oz bean sprouts

45 ml/3 tbsp groundnut (peanut) oil

100 g/4 oz Chinese cabbage, shredded

225 g/8 oz roast pork, sliced

5 ml/1 tsp salt

15 ml/1 tbsp rice wine or dry sherry

Blanch the bean sprouts in boiling water for 4 minutes then drain. Heat the oil and stir-fry the bean sprouts and cabbage until just softened. Add the pork, salt and sherry and stir-fry until heated through. Add half the drained noodles to the pan and stir gently until heated through. Add the remaining noodles and stir until heated through.

Pork with Chutney

Serves 4

5 ml/1 tsp five-spice powder

5 ml/1 tsp curry powder

450 g/1 lb pork, cut into strips

30 ml/2 tbsp groundnut (peanut) oil

6 spring onions (scallions), cut into strips

1 stick celery, cut into strips

100 g/4 oz bean sprouts

1 x 200 g/7 oz jar Chinese sweet pickles, diced

45 ml/3 tbsp mango chutney

30 ml/2 tbsp soy sauce

30 ml/2 tbsp tomato purée (paste)

150 ml/¼ pt/generous ½ cup chicken stock

10 ml/2 tsp cornflour (cornstarch)

Rub the spices well into the pork. Heat the oil and stir-fry the meat for 8 minutes or until cooked. Remove from the pan. Add the vegetables to the pan and stir-fry for 5 minutes. Return the pork to the pan with all the remaining ingredients except the cornflour. Stir until heated through. Mix the cornflour with a little water, stir it into the pan and simmer, stirring, until the sauce thickens.

Pork with Cucumber

Serves 4

225 g/8 oz lean pork, cut into strips
30 ml/2 tbsp plain (all-purpose) flour
salt and freshly ground pepper
60 ml/4 tbsp groundnut (peanut) oil
225 g/8 oz cucumber, peeled and sliced
30 ml/2 tbsp soy sauce

Toss the pork in the flour and season with salt and pepper. Heat the oil and stir-fry the pork for about 5 minutes until cooked. Add the cucumber and soy sauce and stir-fry for a further 4 minutes. Check and adjust the seasoning and serve with fried rice.

Crispy Pork Parcels

Serves 4

4 dried Chinese mushrooms

30 ml/2 tbsp groundnut (peanut) oil

225 g/8 oz pork fillet, minced (ground)

50 g/2 oz peeled prawns, chopped

15 ml/1 tbsp soy sauce

15 ml/1 tbsp cornflour (cornstarch)

30 ml/2 tbsp water

8 spring roll wrappers

100 g/4 oz/1 cup cornflour (cornstarch)

oil for deep-frying

Soak the mushrooms in warm water for 30 minutes then drain. Discard the stalks and finely chop the caps. Heat the oil and fry the mushrooms, pork, prawns and soy sauce for 2 minutes. Blend the cornflour and water to a paste and stir into the mixture to make the filling.

Cut the wrappers into strips, place a little filling on the end of each one and roll up into triangles, sealing with a little flour and water mixture. Dust generously with cornflour. Heat the oil and deep-fry the triangles until crisp and golden brown. Drain well before serving.

Pork Egg Rolls

Serves 4

225 g/8 oz lean pork, shredded

1 slice ginger root, minced

1 spring onion, chopped

15 ml/1 tbsp soy sauce

15 ml/1 tbsp water

12 egg roll skins

1 egg, beaten

oil for deep-frying

Mix together the pork, ginger, onion, soy sauce and water. Place a little of the filling on the centre of each skin and brush the edges with beaten egg. Fold in the sides then roll the egg roll away from you, sealing the edges with egg. Steam on a rack in a steamer for 30 minutes until the pork is cooked. Heat the oil and deep-fry for a few minutes until crisp and golden.

Serves 4

30 ml/2 tbsp groundnut (peanut) oil

225 g/8 oz lean pork, shredded

6 spring onions (scallions), chopped

225 g/8 oz bean sprouts

100 g/4 oz peeled prawns, chopped

15 ml/1 tbsp soy sauce

2.5 ml/½ tsp salt

12 egg roll skins

1 egg, beaten

oil for deep-frying

Heat the oil and fry the pork and spring onions until lightly browned. Meanwhile blanch the bean sprouts in boiling water for 2 minutes then drain. Add the bean sprouts to the pan and stir-fry for 1 minute. Add the prawns, soy sauce and salt and stir-fry for 2 minutes. Leave to cool.

Place a little filling on the centre of each skin and brush the edges with beaten egg. Fold in the sides then roll up the egg rolls, sealing the edges with egg. Heat the oil and deep-fry the egg rolls until crisp and golden.

Braised Pork with Eggs

Serves 4

450 g/1 lb lean pork
30 ml/2 tbsp groundnut (peanut) oil
1 onion, chopped
90 ml/6 tbsp soy sauce
45 ml/3 tbsp rice wine or dry sherry
15 ml/1 tbsp brown sugar
3 hard-boiled (hard-cooked) eggs

Bring a saucepan of water to the boil, add the pork, return to the boil and boil until sealed. Remove from the pan, drain well then cut into cubes. Heat the oil and fry the onion until softened. Add the pork and stir-fry until lightly browned. Stir in the soy sauce, wine or sherry and sugar, cover and simmer for 30 minutes, stirring occasionally. Score the outside of the eggs slightly then add them to the pan, cover and simmer for a further 30 minutes.

Fiery Pork

Serves 4

450 g/1 lb pork fillet, cut into strips

30 ml/2 tbsp soy sauce

30 ml/2 tbsp hoisin sauce

5 ml/1 tsp five-spice powder

15 ml/1 tbsp pepper

15 ml/1 tbsp brown sugar

15 ml/1 tbsp sesame oil

30 ml/2 tbsp groundnut (peanut) oil

6 spring onions (scallions), chopped

1 green pepper, cut into chunks

200 g/7 oz bean sprouts

2 slices pineapple, diced

45 ml/3 tbsp tomato ketchup (catsup)

150 ml/¼ pt/generous ½ cup chicken stock

Place the meat in a bowl. Mix the soy sauce, hoisin sauce, five-spice powder, pepper and sugar, pour over the meat and leave to marinate for 1 hour. Heat the oils and stir-fry the meat until golden brown. Remove from the pan. Add the vegetables and fry for 2 minutes. Add the pineapple, tomato ketchup and stock and bring to the boil. Return the meat to the pan and heat through before serving.

Deep-Fried Pork Fillet

Serves 4

350 g/12 oz pork fillet, cubed
15 ml/1 tbsp rice wine or dry sherry
15 ml/1 tbsp soy sauce
5 ml/1 tsp sesame oil
30 ml/2 tbsp cornflour (cornstarch)
oil for deep-frying

Mix together the pork, wine or sherry, soy sauce, sesame oil and cornflour so that the pork is coated with a thick batter. Heat the oil and deep-fry the pork for about 3 minutes until crisp. Remove the pork from the pan, reheat the oil and deep-fry again for about 3 minutes.

Five-Spice Pork

Serves 4

225 g/8 oz lean pork

5 ml/1 tsp cornflour (cornstarch)

2.5 ml/½ tsp five-spice powder

2.5 ml/½ tsp salt

15 ml/1 tbsp rice wine or dry sherry

20 ml/2 tbsp groundnut (peanut) oil

120 ml/4 fl oz/½ cup chicken stock

Slice the pork thinly against the grain. Mix the pork with the cornflour, five-spice powder, salt and wine or sherry and stir well to coat the pork. Leave to stand for 30 minutes, stirring occasionally. Heat the oil, add the pork and stir-fry for about 3 minutes. Add the stock, bring to the boil, cover and simmer for 3 minutes. Serve immediately.

Braised Fragrant Pork

Serves 6–8

1 piece tangerine peel

45 ml/3 tbsp groundnut (peanut) oil

900 g/2 lb lean pork, cubed

250 ml/8 fl oz/1 cup rice wine or dry sherry

120 ml/4 fl oz/½ cup soy sauce

2.5 ml/½ tsp anise powder

½ cinnamon stick

4 cloves

5 ml/1 tsp salt

250 ml/8 fl oz/1 cup water

2 spring onions (scallions), sliced

1 slice ginger root, chopped

Soak the tangerine peel in water while you prepare the dish. Heat the oil and fry the pork until lightly browned. Add the wine or sherry, soy sauce, anise powder, cinnamon, cloves, salt and water. Bring to the boil, add the tangerine peel, spring onion and ginger. Cover and simmer for about 1½ hours until tender, stirring occasionally and adding a little extra boiling water if necessary. Remove the spices before serving.

Serves 4

450 g/1 lb belly of pork, skinned

3 slices ginger root

2 spring onions (scallions), chopped

30 ml/2 tbsp minced garlic

30 ml/2 tbsp soy sauce

5 ml/1 tsp salt

15 ml/1 tbsp chicken stock

2.5 ml/½ tsp chilli oil

4 sprigs coriander

Place the pork in a pan with the ginger and spring onions, cover with water, bring to the boil and simmer for 30 minutes until cooked through. Remove and drain well, then cut into thin slices about 5 cm/2 in square. Arrange the slices in a metal strainer. Bring a pan of water to the boil, add the pork slices and cook for 3 minutes until heated through. Arrange on a warmed serving plate. Mix together the garlic, soy sauce, salt, stock and chilli oil and spoon over the pork. Serve garnished with coriander.

Stir-Fried Pork with Ginger

Serves 4

225 g/8 oz lean pork

5 ml/1 tsp cornflour (cornstarch)

30 ml/2 tbsp soy sauce

30 ml/2 tbsp groundnut (peanut) oil

1 slice ginger root, minced

1 spring onion (scallion), sliced

45 ml/3 tbsp water

5 ml/1 tsp brown sugar

Slice the pork thinly against the grain. Toss in cornflour then sprinkle with soy sauce and toss again. Heat the oil and stir-fry the pork for 2 minutes until sealed. Add the ginger and spring onion and stir-fry for 1 minute. Add the water and sugar, cover and simmer for about 5 minutes until cooked through.

Pork with Green Beans

Serves 4

450 g/1 lb green beans, cut into chunks

30 ml/2 tbsp groundnut (peanut) oil

2.5 ml/½ tsp salt

1 slice ginger root, minced

225 g/8 oz lean pork, minced (ground)

120 ml/4 fl oz/½ cup chicken stock

75 ml/5 tbsp water

2 eggs

15 ml/1 tbsp cornflour (cornstarch)

Parboil the beans for about 2 minutes then drain. Heat the oil and stir-fry the salt and ginger for a few seconds. Add the pork and stir-fry until lightly browned. Add the beans and stir-fry for 30 seconds, coating with the oil. Stir in the stock, bring to the boil, cover and simmer for 2 minutes. Beat 30 ml/2 tbsp of water with the eggs and stir them into the pan. Mix the remaining water with the cornflour. When the eggs begin to set, stir in the cornflour and cook until the mixture thickens. Serve immediately.

Pork with Ham and Tofu

Serves 4

4 dried Chinese mushrooms

5 ml/1 tsp groundnut (peanut) oil

100 g/4 oz smoked ham, sliced

225 g/8 oz tofu, sliced

225 g/8 oz lean pork, sliced

15 ml/1 tbsp rice wine or dry sherry

salt and freshly ground pepper

1 slice ginger root, chopped

1 spring onion (scallion), chopped

10 ml/2 tsp cornflour (cornstarch)

30 ml/2 tbsp water

Soak the mushrooms in warm water for 30 minutes then drain. Discard the stalks and halve the caps. Rub a heatproof bowl with the groundnut (peanut) oil. Arrange the mushrooms, ham, tofu and pork in layers in the dish, with pork on top. Sprinkle with wine or sherry, salt and pepper, ginger and spring onion. Cover and steam on a rack over boiling water for about 45 minutes until cooked. Drain the gravy from the bowl without disturbing the ingredients. Add enough water to make up 250 ml/8 fl oz/1 cup. Mix together the cornflour and water and stir it into the sauce.

Bring to the bowl and simmer, stirring, until the sauce clears and thickens. Turn the pork mixture on to a warmed serving plate, pour over the sauce and serve.

Fried Pork Kebabs

Serves 4

450 g/1 lb pork fillet, thinly sliced
100 g/4 oz cooked ham, thinly sliced
6 water chestnuts, thinly sliced
30 ml/2 tbsp soy sauce
30 ml/2 tbsp wine vinegar
15 ml/1 tbsp brown sugar
15 ml/1 tbsp oyster sauce
few drops of chilli oil
45 ml/3 tbsp cornflour (cornstarch)
30 ml/2 tbsp rice wine or dry sherry
2 eggs, beaten
oil for deep-frying

Thread the pork, ham and water chestnuts alternately on to small skewers. Mix together the soy sauce, wine vinegar, sugar, oyster sauce and chilli oil. Pour over the kebabs, cover and leave to marinate in the refrigerator for 3 hours. Mix the cornflour, wine or sherry and eggs to a smooth, thickish batter. Twist the kebabs in the batter to coat them. Heat the oil and deep-fry the kebabs until light golden brown.

Braised Pork Knuckle in Red Sauce

Serves 4

1 large knuckle of pork

1 l/1½ pts/4¼ cups boiling water

5 ml/1 tsp salt

120 ml/4 fl oz/½ cup wine vinegar

120 ml/4 fl oz/½ cup soy sauce

45 ml/3 tbsp honey

5 ml/1 tsp juniper berries

5 ml/1 tsp aniseed

5 ml/1 tsp coriander

60 ml/4 tbsp groundnut (peanut) oil

6 spring onions (scallions), sliced

2 carrots, thinly sliced

1 stick celery, sliced

45 ml/3 tbsp hoisin sauce

30 ml/2 tbsp mango chutney

75 ml/5 tbsp tomato purée (paste)

1 clove garlic, crushed

60 ml/4 tbsp chopped chives

Bring the knuckle of pork to the boil with the water, salt, wine vinegar, 45 ml/3 tbsp of soy sauce, the honey and spices. Add the vegetables, bring back to the boil, cover and simmer for about 1½ hours until the meat is tender. Remove the meat and vegetables from the pan, cut the meat off the bone and dice it. Heat the oil and fry the meat until golden brown. Add the vegetables and stir-fry for 5 minutes. Add the remaining soy sauce, the hoisin sauce, chutney, tomato purée and garlic. Bring to the boil, stirring, then simmer for 3 minutes. Serve sprinkled with chives.

Marinated Pork

Serves 4

450 g/1 lb lean pork

1 slice ginger root, minced

1 clove garlic, crushed

90 ml/6 tbsp soy sauce

15 ml/1 tbsp rice wine or dry sherry

45 ml/3 tbsp groundnut (peanut) oil

1 spring onion (scallion), sliced

15 ml/1 tbsp brown sugar

freshly ground pepper

Mix the pork with the ginger, garlic, 30 ml/2 tbsp soy sauce and wine or sherry. Leave to stand for 30 minutes, stirring occasionally, then lift the meat from the marinade. Heat the oil and fry the pork until lightly browned. Add the spring onion, sugar, remaining soy sauce and a pinch of pepper, cover and simmer for about 45 minutes until the pork is cooked. Cut the pork into cubes then serve.

Serves 6

6 pork chops

1 slice ginger root, minced

1 clove garlic, crushed

90 ml/6 tbsp soy sauce

30 ml/2 tbsp rice wine or dry sherry

45 ml/3 tbsp groundnut (peanut) oil

2 spring onions (scallions), chopped

15 ml/1 tbsp brown sugar

freshly ground pepper

Cut the bone from the pork chops and cut the meat into cubes. Mix the ginger, garlic, 30 ml/2 tbsp of soy sauce and the wine or sherry, pour over the pork and leave to marinate for 30 minutes, stirring occasionally. Remove the meat from the marinade. Heat the oil and fry the pork until lightly browned. Add the spring onions and stir-fry for 1 minute. Mix the remaining soy sauce with the sugar and a pinch of pepper. Stir into the sauce, bring to the boil, cover and simmer for about 30 minutes until the pork is tender.

Serves 4

25 g/1 oz dried Chinese mushrooms

30 ml/2 tbsp groundnut (peanut) oil

1 clove garlic, chopped

225 g/8 oz lean pork, cut into slivers

4 spring onions (scallions), chopped

15 ml/1 tbsp soy sauce

15 ml/1 tbsp rice wine or dry sherry

5 ml/1 tsp sesame oil

Soak the mushrooms in warm water for 30 minutes then drain. Discard the stems and slice the caps. Heat the oil and fry the garlic until lightly browned. Add the pork and stir-fry until browned. Stir in the spring onions, mushrooms, soy sauce and wine or sherry and stir-fry for 3 minutes. Stir in the sesame oil and serve immediately.

Steamed Meat Cake

Serves 4

450 g/1 lb minced (ground) pork

4 water chestnuts, finely chopped

225 g/8 oz mushrooms, finely chopped

5 ml/1 tsp soy sauce

salt and freshly ground pepper

1 egg, lightly beaten

Mix all the ingredients together well and shape the mixture into a flat pie on an ovenproof plate. Place the plate on a rack in a steamer, cover and steam for 1½ hours.

Red-Cooked Pork with Mushrooms

Serves 4

450 g/1 lb lean pork, cubed

250 ml/8 fl oz/1 cup water

15 ml/1 tbsp soy sauce

15 ml/1 tbsp rice wine or dry sherry

5 ml/1 tsp sugar

5 ml/1 tsp salt

225 g/8 oz button mushrooms

Place the pork and water in a pan and bring the water to the boil. Cover and simmer for 30 minutes then drain, reserving the stock. Return the pork to the pan and add the soy sauce. Simmer over a low heat, stirring, until the soy sauce is absorbed. Stir in the wine or sherry, sugar and salt. Pour in the reserved stock, bring to the boil, cover and simmer for about 30 minutes, turning the meat occasionally. Add the mushrooms and simmer for a further 20 minutes.

Pork with Noodle Pancake

Serves 4

30 ml/2 tbsp groundnut (peanut) oil

5 ml/2 tsp salt

225 g/8 oz lean pork, cut into strips

225 g/8 oz Chinese cabbage, shredded

100 g/4 oz bamboo shoots, shredded

100 g/4 oz mushrooms, thinly sliced

150 ml/¼ pt/generous ½ cup chicken stock

10 ml/2 tsp cornflour (cornstarch)

15 ml/1 tbsp rice wine or dry sherry

15 ml/1 tbsp water

noodle pancake

Heat the oil and fry the salt and pork until lightly coloured. Add the cabbage, bamboo shoots and mushrooms and stir-fry for 1 minute. Add the stock, bring to the boil, cover and simmer for 4 minutes until the pork is cooked. Mix the cornflour to a paste with the wine or sherry and water, stir it into the pan and simmer, stirring, until the sauce clears and thickens. Pour over the noodle pancake to serve.

Serves 4

30 ml/2 tbsp groundnut (peanut) oil

5 ml/1 tsp salt

4 spring onions (scallions), chopped

1 clove garlic, crushed

225 g/8 oz lean pork, cut into strips

100 g/4 oz mushrooms, sliced

4 stalks celery, sliced

225 g/8 oz peeled prawns

30 ml/2 tbsp soy sauce

10 ml/1 tsp cornflour (cornstarch)

45 ml/3 tbsp water

noodle pancake

Heat the oil and salt and fry the spring onions and garlic until softened. Add the pork and stir-fry until lightly browned. Add the mushrooms and celery and stir-fry for 2 minutes. Add the prawns, sprinkle with soy sauce and stir until heated through. Mix the cornflour and water to a paste, stir into the pan and simmer, stirring, until hot. Pour over the noodle pancake to serve.

Pork with Oyster Sauce

Serves 4–6

450 g/1 lb lean pork

15 ml/1 tbsp cornflour (cornstarch)

10 ml/2 tsp rice wine or dry sherry

pinch of sugar

45 ml/3 tbsp groundnut (peanut) oil

10 ml/2 tsp water

30 ml/2 tbsp oyster sauce

freshly ground pepper

1 slice ginger root, minced

60 ml/4 tbsp chicken stock

Slice the pork thinly against the grain. Mix 5 ml/1 tsp of cornflour with the wine or sherry, sugar and 5 ml/1 tsp of oil, add to the pork and stir well to coat. Blend the remaining cornflour with the water, oyster sauce and a pinch of pepper. Heat the remaining oil and fry the ginger for 1 minute. Add the pork and stir-fry until lightly browned. Add the stock and the water and oyster sauce mixture, bring to the boil, cover and simmer for 3 minutes.

Pork with Peanuts

Serves 4

450 g/1 lb lean pork, cubed

15 ml/1 tbsp cornflour (cornstarch)

5 ml/1 tsp salt

1 egg white

3 spring onions (scallions), chopped

1 clove garlic, chopped

1 slice ginger root, chopped

45 ml/3 tbsp chicken stock

15 ml/1 tbsp rice wine or dry sherry

15 ml/1 tbsp soy sauce

10 ml/2 tsp black treacle

45 ml/3 tbsp groundnut (peanut) oil

½ cucumber, cubed

25 g/1 oz/¼ cup shelled peanuts

5 ml/1 tsp chilli oil

Mix the pork with half the cornflour, the salt and egg white and stir well to coat the pork. Mix the remaining cornflour with the spring onions, garlic, ginger, stock, wine or sherry, soy sauce and treacle. Heat the oil and stir-fry the pork until lightly browned then remove it from the pan. Add the cucumber to the pan and stir-fry for a few minutes. Return the pork to the pan and stir lightly. Stir in the seasoning mixture, bring to the boil and simmer, stirring, until the sauce clears and thickens. Stir in the peanuts and chilli oil and heat through before serving.

Pork with Peppers

Serves 4

45 ml/3 tbsp groundnut (peanut) oil

225 g/8 oz lean pork, cubed

1 onion, diced

2 green peppers, diced

½ head Chinese leaves, diced

1 slice ginger root, minced

15 ml/1 tbsp soy sauce

15 ml/1 tbsp sugar

2.5 ml/½ tsp salt

Heat the oil and stir-fry the pork for about 4 minutes until golden brown. Add the onion and stir-fry for about 1 minute. Add the peppers and stir-fry for 1 minute. Add the Chinese leaves and stir-fry for 1 minute. Mix together the remaining ingredients, stir them into the pan and stir-fry for a further 2 minutes.

Spicy Pork with Pickles

Serves 4

900 g/2 lb pork chops

30 ml/2 tbsp cornflour (cornstarch)

45 ml/3 tbsp soy sauce

30 ml/2 tbsp sweet sherry

5 ml/1 tsp grated ginger root

2.5 ml/½ tsp five-spice powder

pinch of freshly ground pepper

oil for deep-frying

60 ml/4 tbsp chicken stock

Chinese pickled vegetables

Trim the chops, discarding all the fat and bones. Mix together the cornflour, 30 ml/2 tbsp of soy sauce, the sherry, ginger, five-spice powder and pepper. Pour over the pork and stir to coat it completely. Cover and leave to marinate for 2 hours, turning occasionally. Heat the oil and deep-fry the pork until golden brown and cooked through. Drain on kitchen paper. Cut the pork into thick slices, transfer to a warmed serving dish and keep warm. Mix together the stock and remaining soy sauce in a small pan. Bring to the boil and pour over the sliced pork. Serve garnished with mixed pickles.

Pork with Plum Sauce

Serves 4

450 g/1 lb stewing pork, diced

2 cloves garlic, crushed

salt

60 ml/4 tbsp tomato ketchup (catsup)

30 ml/2 tbsp soy sauce

45 ml/3 tbsp plum sauce

5 ml/1 tsp curry powder

5 ml/1 tsp paprika

2.5 ml/½ tsp freshly ground pepper

45 ml/3 tbsp groundnut (peanut) oil

6 spring onions (scallions), cut into strips

4 carrots, cut into strips

Marinate the meat with the garlic, salt, tomato ketchup, soy sauce, plum sauce, curry powder, paprika and pepper for 30 minutes. Heat the oil and fry the meat until lightly browned. Remove from the wok. Add the vegetables to the oil and fry until just tender. Return the meat to the pan and reheat gently before serving.

Serves 6–8

900 g/2 lb lean pork

30 ml/2 tbsp groundnut (peanut) oil

1 onion, sliced

1 spring onion (scallion), chopped

2 cloves garlic, crushed

30 ml/2 tbsp soy sauce

50 g/2 oz peeled prawns, minced

(ground)

600 ml/1 pt/2½ cups boiling water

15 ml/1 tbsp sugar

Bring a saucepan of water to the boil, add the pork, cover and simmer for 10 minutes. Remove from the pan and drain well then cut into cubes. Heat the oil and fry the onion, spring onion and garlic until lightly browned. Add the pork and fry until lightly browned. Add the soy sauce and prawns and stir-fry for 1 minute. Add the boiling water and sugar, cover and simmer for about 40 minutes until the pork is tender.

Red-Cooked Pork

Serves 4

675 g/1½ lb lean pork, cubed

250 ml/8 fl oz/1 cup water

1 slice ginger root, crushed

60 ml/4 tbsp soy sauce

15 ml/1 tbsp rice wine or dry sherry

5 ml/1 tsp salt

10 ml/2 tsp brown sugar

Place the pork and water in a pan and bring the water to the boil. Add the ginger, soy sauce, sherry and salt, cover and simmer for 45 minutes. Add the sugar, turn the meat over, cover and simmer for a further 45 minutes until the pork is tender.

Pork in Red Sauce

Serves 4

30 ml/2 tbsp groundnut (peanut) oil

225 g/8 oz pork kidneys, cut into strips

450 g/1 lb pork, cut into strips

1 onion, sliced

4 spring onions (scallions), cut into strips

2 carrots, cut into strips

1 stick celery, cut into strips

1 red pepper, cut into strips

45 ml/3 tbsp soy sauce

45 ml/3 tbsp dry white wine

300 ml/½ pt/1¼ cups chicken stock

30 ml/2 tbsp plum sauce

30 ml/2 tbsp wine vinegar

5 ml/1 tsp five-spice powder

5 ml/1 tsp brown sugar

15 ml/1 tbsp cornflour (cornstarch)

15 ml/1 tbsp water

Heat the oil and fry the kidneys for 2 minutes then remove them from the pan. Reheat the oil and fry the pork until lightly browned. Add the vegetables and stir-fry for 3 minutes. Add the soy sauce, wine, stock, plum sauce, wine vinegar, five-spice powder and sugar, bring to the boil, cover and simmer for 30 minutes until cooked. Add the kidneys. Mix together the cornflour and water and stir into the pan. Bring to the boil then simmer, stirring, until the sauce thickens.

Pork with Rice Noodles

Serves 4

4 dried Chinese mushrooms

100 g/4 oz rice noodles

225 g/8 oz lean pork, cut into strips

15 ml/1 tbsp cornflour (cornstarch)

15 ml/1 tbsp soy sauce

15 ml/1 tbsp rice wine or dry sherry

45 ml/3 tbsp groundnut (peanut) oil

2.5 ml/½ tsp salt

1 slice ginger root, minced

2 stalks celery, chopped

120 ml/4 fl oz/½ cup chicken stock

2 spring onions (scallions), sliced

Soak the mushrooms in warm water for 30 minutes then drain. Discard and stalks and slice the caps. Soak the noodles in warm water for 30 minutes then drain and cut into 5 cm/2 in pieces. Place the pork in a bowl. Mix together the cornflour, soy sauce and wine or sherry, pour over the pork and toss to coat. Heat the oil and fry the salt and ginger for a few seconds. Add the pork and stir-fry until lightly browned. Add the mushrooms and celery and stir-fry for 1 minute. Add the stock, bring to the boil, cover and simmer for 2 minutes. Add and noodles and heat through for 2 minutes. Stir in the spring onions and serve at once.

Rich Pork Balls

Serves 4

450 g/1 lb minced (ground) pork

100 g/4 oz tofu, mashed

4 water chestnuts, finely chopped

salt and freshly ground pepper

120 ml/4 fl oz/½ cup groundnut (peanut) oil

1 slice ginger root, minced

600 ml/1 pt/2½ cups chicken stock

15 ml/1 tbsp soy sauce

5 ml/1 tsp brown sugar

5 ml/1 tsp rice wine or dry sherry

Mix the pork, tofu and chestnuts and season with salt and pepper. Shape into large balls. Heat the oil and fry the pork balls until golden brown on all sides then remove from the pan. Drain off all but 15 ml/1 tbsp of the oil and add the ginger, stock, soy sauce, sugar and wine or sherry. Return the pork balls to the pan, bring to the boil and simmer gently for 20 minutes until cooked through.

Roast Pork Chops

Serves 4

4 pork chops

75 ml/5 tbsp soy sauce

oil for deep-frying

100 g/4 oz celery sticks

3 spring onions (scallions), chopped

1 slice ginger root, chopped

15 ml/1 tbsp rice wine or dry sherry

120 ml/4 fl oz/½ cup chicken stock

salt and freshly ground pepper

5 ml/1 tsp sesame oil

Dip the pork chops in the soy sauce until they are well coated. Heat the oil and deep-fry the chops until golden brown. Remove and drain well. Arrange the celery in the base of a shallow ovenproof dish. Sprinkle with the spring onions and ginger and arrange the pork chops on top. Pour over the wine or sherry and stock and season with salt and pepper. Sprinkle with sesame oil. Roast in a preheated oven at 200°C/400°C/gas mark 6 for 15 minutes.

Spiced Pork

Serves 4

1 cucumber, cubed

salt

450 g/1 lb lean pork, cubed

5 ml/1 tsp salt

45 ml/3 tbsp soy sauce

30 ml/2 tbsp rice wine or dry sherry

30 ml/2 tbsp cornflour (cornstarch)

15 ml/1 tbsp brown sugar

60 ml/4 tbsp groundnut (peanut) oil

1 slice ginger root, chopped

1 clove garlic, chopped

1 red chilli pepper, seeded and chopped

60 ml/4 tbsp chicken stock

Sprinkle the cucumber with salt and leave to one side. Mix together the pork, salt, 15 ml/1 tbsp of soy sauce, 15 ml/1 tbsp of wine or sherry, 15 ml/ 1 tbsp of cornflour, the brown sugar and 15 ml/1 tbsp of oil. Leave to stand for 30 minutes then lift the meat from the marinade. Heat the remaining oil and stir-fry the pork until lightly browned. Add the ginger, garlic and chilli and stir-fry for 2 minutes. Add the cucumber and stir-fry for 2 minutes. Mix the stock and remaining soy sauce, wine or sherry and cornflour into the marinade. Stir this into the pan and bring to the boil, stirring. Simmer, stirring, until the sauce clears and thickens and continue to simmer until the meat is cooked through.

Slippery Pork Slices

Serves 4

225 g/8 oz lean pork, sliced
2 egg whites
15 ml/1 tbsp cornflour (cornstarch)
45 ml/3 tbsp groundnut (peanut) oil
50 g/2 oz bamboo shoots, sliced
6 spring onions (scallions), chopped
2.5 ml/½ tsp salt
15 ml/1 tbsp rice wine or dry sherry
150 ml/¼ pt/generous ½ cup chicken stock

Toss the pork with the egg whites and cornflour until well coated. Heat the oil and stir-fry the pork until lightly browned then remove it from the pan. Add the bamboo shoots and spring onions and stir-fry for 2 minutes. Return the pork to the pan with the salt, wine or sherry and chicken stock. Bring to the boil and simmer, stirring for 4 minutes until the pork is cooked.

Pork with Spinach and Carrots

Serves 4

225 g/8 oz lean pork

2 carrots, cut into strips

225 g/8 oz spinach

45 ml/3 tbsp groundnut (peanut) oil

1 spring onion (scallion), finely chopped

15 ml/1 tbsp soy sauce

2.5 ml/½ tsp salt

10 ml/2 tsp cornflour (cornstarch)

30 ml/2 tbsp water

Slice the pork thinly against the grain then cut it into strips. Parboil the carrots for about 3 minutes then drain. Halve the spinach leaves. Heat the oil and fry the spring onion until translucent. Add the pork and stir-fry until lightly browned. Add the carrots and soy sauce and stir-fry for 1 minute. Add the salt and spinach and stir-fry for about 30 seconds until it begins to soften. Mix the cornflour and water to a paste, stir it into the sauce and stir-fry until it clears then serve at once.

Steamed Pork

Serves 4

450 g/1 lb lean pork, cubed
120 ml/4 fl oz/½ cup soy sauce
120 ml/4 fl oz/½ cup rice wine or dry sherry
15 ml/1 tbsp brown sugar

Mix together all the ingredients and place in a heatproof bowl. Steam on a rack over boiling water for about 1½ hours until cooked through.

Stir-Fried Pork

Serves 4

25 g/1 oz dried Chinese mushrooms

15 ml/1 tbsp groundnut (peanut) oil

450 g/1 lb lean pork, sliced

1 green pepper, diced

15 ml/1 tbsp soy sauce

15 ml/1 tbsp rice wine or dry sherry

5 ml/1 tsp salt

5 ml/1 tsp sesame oil

Soak the mushrooms in warm water for 30 minutes then drain. Discard the stems and slice the caps. Heat the oil and stir-fry the pork until lightly browned. Add the pepper and stir-fry for 1 minute. Add the mushrooms, soy sauce, wine or sherry and salt and stir-fry for a few minutes until the meat is cooked. Stir in the sesame oil before serving.

Pork with Sweet Potatoes

Serves 4

oil for deep-frying

2 large sweet potatoes, sliced

30 ml/2 tbsp groundnut (peanut) oil

1 slice ginger root, sliced

1 onion, sliced

450 g/1 lb lean pork, cubed

15 ml/1 tbsp soy sauce

2.5 ml/½ tsp salt

freshly ground pepper

250 ml/8 fl oz/1 cup chicken stock

30 ml/2 tbsp curry powder

Heat the oil and deep-fry the sweet potatoes until golden. Remove from the pan and drain well. Heat the groundnut (peanut) oil and fry the ginger and onion until lightly browned. Add the pork and stir-fry until lightly browned. Add the soy sauce, salt and a pinch of pepper then stir in the stock and curry powder, bring to the boil and simmer, stirring for 1 minute. Add the fried potatoes, cover and simmer for 30 minutes until the pork is cooked.

Serves 4

450 g/1 lb lean pork, cubed

15 ml/1 tbsp rice wine or dry sherry

15 ml/1 tbsp groundnut (peanut) oil

5 ml/1 tsp curry powder

1 egg, beaten

salt

100 g/4 oz cornflour (cornstarch)

oil for deep-frying

1 clove garlic, crushed

75 g/3 oz/½ cup sugar

50 g/2 oz tomato ketchup (catsup)

5 ml/1 tsp wine vinegar

5 ml/1 tsp sesame oil

Mix the pork with the wine or sherry, oil, curry powder, egg and a little salt. Mix in the cornflour until the pork is covered with the batter. Heat the oil until smoking then add the pork cubes a few a time. Fry for about 3 minutes then drain and set aside. Reheat the oil and fry the cubes again for about 2 minutes. Remove and drain. Heat the garlic, sugar, tomato ketchup and wine vinegar, stirring until the sugar dissolves. Bring to the boil then add the pork cubes and stir well. Stir in the sesame oil and serve.

Savoury Pork

Serves 4

30 ml/2 tbsp groundnut (peanut) oil

450 g/1 lb lean pork, cubed

3 spring onions (scallions), sliced

2 cloves garlic, crushed

1 slice ginger root, minced

250 ml/8 fl oz/1 cup soy sauce

30 ml/2 tbsp rice wine or dry sherry

30 ml/2 tbsp brown sugar

5 ml/1 tsp salt

600 ml/1 pt/2½ cups water

Heat the oil and fry the pork until golden brown. Drain off any excess oil, add the spring onions, garlic and ginger and fry for 2 minutes. Add the soy sauce, wine or sherry, sugar and salt and stir well. Add the water, bring to the boil, cover and simmer for 1 hour.

Pork with Tofu

Serves 4

450 g/1 lb lean pork

45 ml/3 tbsp groundnut (peanut) oil

1 onion, sliced

1 clove garlic, crushed

225 g/8 oz tofu, cubed

375 ml/13 fl oz/1½ cups chicken stock

15 ml/1 tbsp brown sugar

60 ml/4 tbsp soy sauce

2.5 ml/½ tsp salt

Place the pork in a saucepan and cover with water. Bring to the boil then simmer for 5 minutes. Drain and leave to cool then cut into cubes.

Heat the oil and fry the onion and garlic until lightly browned. Add the pork and fry until lightly browned. Add the tofu and stir gently until coated with oil. Add the stock, sugar, soy sauce and salt, bring to the boil, cover and simmer for about 40 minutes until the pork is tender.

Soft-Fried Pork

Serves 4

225 g/8 oz pork fillet, cubed
1 egg white
30 ml/2 tbsp rice wine or dry sherry
salt
225 g/8 oz cornflour (cornstarch)
oil for deep-frying

Mix the pork with the egg white, wine or sherry and a little salt. Gradually work in enough cornflour to make a thick batter. Heat the oil and fry the pork until golden brown and crisp outside and tender inside.

Twice-Cooked Pork

Serves 4

225 g/8 oz lean pork
45 ml/3 tbsp groundnut (peanut) oil
2 green peppers, cut into chunks
2 cloves garlic, chopped
2 spring onions (scallions), sliced
15 ml/1 tbsp hot bean sauce
15 ml/1 tbsp chicken stock
5 ml/1 tsp sugar

Place the piece of pork in a pan, cover with water, bring to the boil and simmer for 20 minutes until cooked through. Remove and drain then leave to cool. Slice thinly.

Heat the oil and stir-fry the pork until lightly browned. Add the peppers, garlic and spring onions and stir-fry for 2 minutes. Remove from the pan. Add the bean sauce, stock and sugar to the pan and simmer, stirring, for 2 minutes. Return the pork and peppers and stir-fry until heated through. Serve at once.

Pork with Vegetables

Serves 4

2 cloves garlic, crushed

5 ml/1 tsp salt

2.5 ml/½ tsp freshly ground pepper

30 ml/2 tbsp groundnut (peanut) oil

30 ml/2 tbsp soy sauce

225 g/8 oz broccoli florets

200 g/7 oz cauliflower florets

1 red pepper, diced

1 onion, chopped

2 oranges, peeled and diced

1 piece stem ginger, chopped

30 ml/2 tbsp cornflour (cornstarch)

300 ml/½ pt/1¼ cups water

20 ml/2 tbsp wine vinegar

15 ml/1 tbsp honey

pinch of ground ginger

2.5 ml/½ tsp cumin

Crush the garlic, salt and pepper into the meat. Heat the oil and stir-fry meat until lightly browned. Remove from the pan. Add the soy sauce and vegetables to the pan and stir-fry until tender but still crisp. Add the oranges and ginger. Mix the cornflour and water and stir it into the pan with the wine vinegar, honey, ginger and cumin. Bring to the boil and simmer, stirring, for 2 minutes. Return the pork to the pan and heat through before serving.

Pork with Walnuts

Serves 4

50 g/2 oz/½ cup walnuts
225 g/8 oz lean pork, cut into strips
30 ml/2 tbsp plain (all-purpose) flour
30 ml/2 tbsp brown sugar
30 ml/2 tbsp soy sauce
oil for deep-frying
15 ml/1 tbsp groundnut (peanut) oil

Blanch the walnuts in boiling water for 2 minutes then drain. Mix the pork with the flour, sugar and 15 ml/ 1 tbsp of soy sauce until well coated. Heat the oil and deep-fry the pork until crispy and golden. Drain on kitchen paper. Heat the groundnut (peanut) oil and stir-fry the walnuts until golden. Add the pork to the pan, sprinkle with the remaining soy sauce and stir-fry until heated through.

Pork Wontons

Serves 4

450 g/1 lb minced (ground) pork

1 spring onion (scallion), chopped

225 g/8 oz mixed vegetables, chopped

30 ml/2 tbsp soy sauce

5 ml/1 tsp salt

40 wonton skins

oil for deep-frying

Heat a pan and fry the pork and spring onion until lightly browned. Remove from the heat and stir in the vegetables, soy sauce and salt.

To fold the wontons, hold the skin in the palm of your left hand and spoon a little filling into the centre. Moisten the edges with egg and fold the skin into a triangle, sealing the edges. Moisten the corners with egg and twist them together.

Heat the oil and fry the wontons a few at a time until golden brown. Drain well before serving.

Pork with Water Chestnuts

Serves 4

45 ml/3 tbsp groundnut (peanut) oil

1 clove garlic, crushed

1 spring onion (scallion), chopped

1 slice ginger root, minced

225 g/8 oz lean pork, cut into strips

100 g/4 oz water chestnuts, thinly sliced

45 ml/3 tbsp soy sauce

15 ml/1 tbsp rice wine or dry sherry

5 ml/1 tsp cornflour (cornstarch)

Heat the oil and fry the garlic, spring onion and ginger until lightly browned. Add the pork and stir-fry for 10 minutes until golden brown. Add the water chestnuts and stir-fry for 3 minutes. Add the remaining ingredients and stir-fry for 3 minutes.

Pork and Prawn Wontons

Serves 4

225 g/8 oz minced (ground) pork

2 spring onions (scallions), chopped

100 g/4 oz mixed vegetables, chopped

100 g/4 oz mushrooms, chopped

225 g/8 oz peeled prawns, chopped

15 ml/1 tbsp soy sauce

2.5 ml/½ tsp salt

40 wonton skins

oil for deep-frying

Heat a pan and fry the pork and spring onions until lightly browned. Stir in the remaining ingredients.

To fold the wontons, hold the skin in the palm of your left hand and spoon a little filling into the centre. Moisten the edges with egg and fold the skin into a triangle, sealing the edges. Moisten the corners with egg and twist them together.

Heat the oil and fry the wontons a few at a time until golden brown. Drain well before serving.

Steamed Minced Meatballs

Serves 4

2 cloves garlic, crushed

2.5 ml/½ tsp salt

450 g/1 lb minced (ground) pork

1 onion, chopped

1 red pepper, chopped

1 green pepper, chopped

2 pieces stem ginger, chopped

5 ml/1 tsp curry powder

5 ml/1 tsp paprika

1 egg, beaten

45 ml/3 tbsp cornflour (cornstarch)

50 g/2 oz short-grain rice

salt and freshly ground pepper

60 ml/4 tbsp chopped chives

Mix together the garlic, salt, pork, onion, peppers, ginger, curry powder and paprika. Work the egg into the mixture with the cornflour and rice. Season with salt and pepper then mix in the chives. With wet hands, shape the mixture into small balls. Place these in a steam basket, cover and cook over gently boiling water for 20 minutes until cooked.

Spare Ribs with Black Bean Sauce

Serves 4

900 g/2 lb pork spare ribs

2 cloves garlic, crushed

2 spring onions (scallions), chopped

30 ml/2 tbsp black bean sauce

30 ml/2 tbsp rice wine or dry sherry

15 ml/1 tbsp water

30 ml/2 tbsp soy sauce

15 ml/1 tbsp cornflour (cornstarch)

5 ml/1 tsp sugar

120 ml/4 fl oz½ cup water

30 ml/2 tbsp oil

2.5 ml/½ tsp salt

120 ml/4 fl oz/½ cup chicken stock

Cut the spare ribs into 2.5 cm/1 in pieces. Mix the garlic, spring onions, black bean sauce, wine or sherry, water and 15 ml/1 tbsp of soy sauce. Mix the remaining soy sauce with the cornflour, sugar and water. Heat the oil and salt and fry the spare ribs until golden brown. Drain off the oil. Add the garlic mixture and stir-fry for 2 minutes. Add the stock, bring to the boil, cover and simmer for 4 minutes. Stir in the cornflour mixture and simmer, stirring, until the sauce clears and thickens.

Barbecued Spare Ribs

Serves 4

3 cloves garlic, crushed
75 ml/5 tbsp soy sauce
60 ml/4 tbsp hoisin sauce
60 ml/4 tbsp rice wine or dry sherry
45 ml/3 tbsp brown sugar
30 ml/2 tbsp tomato purée (paste)
900 g/2 lb pork spare ribs
15 ml/1 tbsp honey

Mix the garlic, soy sauce, hoisin sauce, wine or sherry, brown sugar and tomato purée, pour over the ribs, cover and leave to marinate overnight.

Drain the ribs and arrange them on a rack in a roasting tin with a little water underneath. Roast in a preheated oven at 180°C/350°F/gas mark 4 for 45 minutes, basting occasionally with the marinade, reserving 30 ml/2 tbsp of the marinade. Mix the reserved marinade with the honey and brush over the ribs. Barbecue or grill (broil) under a hot grill for about 10 minutes.

Barbecued Maple Spare Ribs

Serves 4

900 g/2 lb pork spare ribs

60 ml/4 tbsp maple syrup

5 ml/1 tsp salt

5 ml/1 tsp sugar

45 ml/3 tbsp soy sauce

15 ml/1 tbsp rice wine or dry sherry

1 clove garlic, crushed

Chop the spare ribs into 5 cm/2 in pieces and place in a bowl. Mix together all the ingredients, add the spare ribs and stir well. Cover and leave to marinate overnight. Grill (broil) or barbecue over a medium heat for about 30 minutes.

Deep-Fried Spare Ribs

Serves 4

900 g/2 lb pork spare ribs

120 ml/4 fl oz/½ cup tomato ketchup (catsup)

120 ml/4 fl oz/½ cup wine vinegar

60 ml/4 tbsp mango chutney

45 ml/3 tbsp rice wine or dry sherry

2 cloves garlic, chopped

5 ml/1 tsp salt

45 ml/3 tbsp soy sauce

30 ml/2 tbsp honey

15 ml/1 tbsp mild curry powder

15 ml/1 tbsp paprika

oil for deep-frying

60 ml/4 tbsp chopped chives

Place the spare ribs in a bowl. Mix together all the ingredients except the oil and chives, pour over the ribs, cover and leave to marinate for at least 1 hour. Heat the oil and deep-fry the ribs until crisp. Serve sprinkled with chives.

Serves 4

450 g/1 lb pork spare ribs

oil for deep-frying

250 ml/8 fl oz/1 cup stock

30 ml/2 tbsp tomato ketchup (catsup)

2.5 ml/½ tsp salt

2.5 ml/½ tsp sugar

2 leeks, cut into chunks

6 spring onions (scallions), cut into chunks

50 g/2 oz broccoli florets

5 ml/1 tsp sesame oil

Chop the spare ribs into 5 cm/2 in chunks. Heat the oil and deep-fry the spare ribs until just beginning to brown. Remove them from the pan and pour off all but 30 ml/2 tbsp of oil. Add the stock, tomato ketchup, salt and sugar, bring to the boil and simmer for 1 minute. Return the spare ribs to the pan and simmer for about 20 minutes until tender.

Meanwhile, heat a further 30 ml/ 2 tbsp of oil and fry the leeks, spring onions and broccoli for about 5 minutes. Sprinkle with sesame oil and arrange round a warmed serving plate. Spoon the spare ribs and sauce into the centre and serve.

Serves 4–6

6 dried Chinese mushrooms

900 g/2 lb pork spare ribs

2 cloves star anise

45 ml/3 tbsp soy sauce

5 ml/1 tsp salt

15 ml/1 tbsp cornflour (cornstarch)

Soak the mushrooms in warm water for 30 minutes then drain. Discard and stalks and slice the caps. Chop the spare ribs into 5 cm/2 in pieces. Bring a pan of water to the boil, add the spare ribs and simmer for 15 minutes. Drain well. Return the ribs to the pan and cover with cold water. Add the mushrooms, star anise, soy sauce and salt. Bring to the boil, cover and simmer for about 45 minutes until the meat is tender. Mix the cornflour with a little cold water, stir it into the pan and simmer, stirring, until the sauce clears and thickens.

Spare Ribs with Orange

Serves 4

900 g/2 lb pork spare ribs

5 ml/1 tsp grated cheese

5 ml/1 tsp cornflour (cornstarch)

45 ml/3 tbsp rice wine or dry sherry

salt

oil for deep-frying

15 ml/1 tbsp water

2.5 ml/½ tsp sugar

15 ml/1 tbsp tomato purée (paste)

2.5 ml/½ tsp chilli sauce

grated rind of 1 orange

1 orange, sliced

Chop the spare ribs into chunks and mix with the cheese, cornflour, 5 ml/ 1 tsp wine or sherry and a pinch of salt. Leave to marinate for 30 minutes. Heat the oil and deep-fry the ribs for about 3 minutes until golden brown. Heat 15 ml/1 tbsp of oil in a wok, add the water, sugar, tomato purée, chilli sauce, orange rind and remaining wine or sherry and stir over a gently heat for 2 minutes. Add the pork and stir together until well coated.

Transfer to a warmed serving plate and serve garnished with orange slices.

Pineapple Spare Ribs

Serves 4

900 g/2 lb pork spare ribs

600 ml/1 pt/2½ cups water

30 ml/2 tbsp groundnut (peanut) oil

2 cloves garlic, finely chopped

200 g/7 oz canned pineapple chunks in fruit juice

120 ml/4 fl oz/½ cup chicken stock

60 ml/4 tbsp wine vinegar

50 g/2 oz/¼ cup brown sugar

15 ml/1 tbsp soy sauce

15 ml/1 tbsp cornflour (cornstarch)

3 spring onions (scallions), chopped

Place the pork and water in a pan, bring to the boil, cover and simmer for 20 minutes. Drain well.

Heat the oil and fry the garlic until lightly browned. Add the ribs and stir-fry until well coated in the oil. Drain the pineapple chunks and add 120 ml/4 fl oz/½ cup of juice to the pan with the stock, wine vinegar, sugar and soy sauce. Bring to the boil, cover and simmer for 10 minutes. Add the drained pineapple. Mix the cornflour with a little water, stir it into the sauce and simmer, stirring, until the sauce clears and thickens. Serve sprinkled with spring onions.

Crispy Prawn Spare Ribs

Serves 4

900 g/2 lb pork spare ribs
450 g/1 lb peeled prawns
5 ml/1 tsp sugar
salt and freshly ground pepper
30 ml/2 tbsp plain (all-purpose) flour
1 egg, lightly beaten
100 g/4 oz breadcrumbs
oil for deep-frying

Cut the spare ribs into 5 cm/2 in chunks. Trim off a little of the meat and mince it with the prawns, sugar, salt and pepper. Stir in the flour and enough egg to make the mixture sticky. Press round the pieces of spare rib then sprinkle them with breadcrumbs. Heat the oil and deep-fry the spare ribs until they come to the surface. Drain well and serve hot.

Serves 4

900 g/2 lb pork spare ribs

450 ml/¾ pt/2 cups water

60 ml/4 tbsp soy sauce

5 ml/1 tsp salt

30 ml/2 tbsp rice wine

5 ml/1 tsp sugar

Cut the ribs into 2.5 cm/1 in pieces. Place in a pan with the water, soy sauce and salt, bring to the boil, cover and simmer for 1 hour. Drain well. Heat a pan and add the spare ribs, rice wine and sugar. Stir-fry over a high heat until the liquid evaporates.

Serves 4

900 g/2 lb pork spare ribs

1 egg

30 ml/2 tbsp plain (all-purpose) flour

5 ml/1 tsp potato flour

45 ml/3 tbsp water

oil for deep-frying

30 ml/2 tbsp groundnut (peanut) oil

30 ml/2 tbsp tomato ketchup (catsup)

30 ml/2 tbsp brown sugar

10 ml/2 tsp wine vinegar

45 ml/3 tbsp sesame seeds

4 lettuce leaves

Chop the spare ribs into 10 cm/4 in pieces and place in a bowl. Mix the egg with the flour, potato flour and water, stir into the spare ribs and leave to stand for 4 hours.

Heat the oil and deep-fry the spare ribs until golden then remove and drain. Heat the oil and fry the tomato ketchup, brown sugar, wine vinegar for a few minutes. Add the spare ribs and stir-fry until thoroughly coated. Sprinkle with sesame seeds and stir-fry for 1 minutes. Arrange the lettuce leaves on a warmed serving plate, top with the spare ribs and serve.

Sweet and Sour Spare Ribs

Serves 4

900 g/2 lb pork spare ribs

600 ml/1 pt/2½ cups water

30 ml/2 tbsp groundnut (peanut) oil

2 cloves garlic, crushed

5 ml/1 tsp salt

100 g/4 oz/½ cup brown sugar

75 ml/5 tbsp chicken stock

60 ml/4 tbsp wine vinegar

100 g/4 oz canned pineapple chunks in syrup

15 ml/1 tbsp tomato purée (paste)

15 ml/1 tbsp soy sauce

15 ml/1 tbsp cornflour (cornstarch)

30 ml/2 tbsp desiccated coconut

Place the pork and water in a pan, bring to the boil, cover and simmer for 20 minutes. Drain well.

Heat the oil and fry the ribs with the garlic and salt until browned. Add the sugar, stock and wine vinegar and bring to the boil. Drain the pineapple and add 30 ml/2 tbsp of the syrup to the pan with the tomato purée, soy sauce and cornflour. Stir well and simmer, stirring, until the sauce clears and thickens. Add the pineapple, simmer for 3 minutes and serve sprinkled with coconut.

Sautéed Spare Ribs

Serves 4

900 g/2 lb pork spare ribs

1 egg, beaten

5 ml/1 tsp soy sauce

5 ml/1 tsp salt

10 ml/2 tsp cornflour (cornstarch)

10 ml/2 tsp sugar

60 ml/4 tbsp groundnut (peanut) oil

250 ml/8 fl oz/1 cup wine vinegar

250 ml/8 fl oz/1 cup water

250 ml/8 fl oz/1 cup rice wine or dry sherry

Place the spare ribs in a bowl. Mix the egg with the soy sauce, salt, half the cornflour and half the sugar, add to the spare ribs and stir well. Heat the oil and fry the spare ribs until browned. Add the remaining ingredients, bring to the boil and simmer until the liquid has almost evaporated.

Spare Ribs with Tomato

Serves 4

900 g/2 lb pork spare ribs

75 ml/5 tbsp soy sauce

30 ml/2 tbsp rice wine or dry sherry

2 eggs, beaten

45 ml/3 tbsp cornflour (cornstarch)

oil for deep-frying

45 ml/3 tbsp groundnut (peanut) oil

1 onion, thinly sliced

250 ml/8 fl oz/1 cup chicken stock

60 ml/4 tbsp tomato ketchup (catsup)

10 ml/2 tsp brown sugar

Cut the spare ribs into 2.5 cm/1 in pieces. Mix with 60 ml/4 tbsp of soy sauce and the wine or sherry and leave to marinate for 1 hour, stirring occasionally. Drain, discarding marinade. Coat the spare ribs in egg then in cornflour. Heat the oil and deep-fry the ribs, a few at a time, until golden. Drain well. Heat the groundnut (peanut) oil and fry the onion until translucent. Add the stock, remaining soy sauce, ketchup and brown sugar and simmer for 1 minute, stirring. Add the ribs and simmer for 10 minutes.

Barbecue-Roast Pork

Serves 4–6

1.25 kg/3 lb boned pork shoulder
2 cloves garlic, crushed
2 spring onions (scallions), chopped
250 ml/8 fl oz/1 cup soy sauce
120 ml/4 fl oz/½ cup rice wine or dry sherry
100 g/4 oz/½ cup brown sugar
5 ml/1 tsp salt

Place the pork in a bowl. Mix together the remaining ingredients, pour over the pork, cover and leave to marinate for 3 hours. Transfer the pork and marinade to a roasting tin and roast in a preheated oven at 200°C/400°F/gas mark 6 for 10 minutes. Reduce the temperature to 160°C/325°F/gas mark 3 for 1¾ hours until the pork is cooked.

Cold Pork with Mustard

Serves 4

1 kg/2 lb boned roasting pork

250 ml/8 fl oz/1 cup soy sauce

120 ml/4 fl oz/½ cup rice wine or dry sherry

100 g/4 oz/½ cup brown sugar

3 spring onions (scallions), chopped

5 ml/1 tsp salt

30 ml/2 tbsp mustard powder

Place the pork in a bowl. Mix all the remaining ingredients except the mustard and pour over the pork. Leave to marinate for at least 2 hours, basting frequently. Line a roasting tin with foil and stand the pork on a rack in the tin. Roast in a preheated oven at 200°C/400°F/gas mark 6 for 10 minutes then reduce the temperature to 160°C/325°F/gas mark 3 for a further 1¾ hours until the pork is tender. Leave to cool then chill in the refrigerator. Slice very thinly. Mix the mustard powder with just enough water to make a creamy paste to serve with the pork.

Serves 6

1.25 kg/3 lb joint of pork, thickly sliced

2 cloves garlic, finely chopped

30 ml/2 tbsp rice wine or dry sherry

15 ml/1 tbsp brown sugar

15 ml/1 tbsp honey

90 ml/6 tbsp soy sauce

2.5 ml/½ tsp five-spice powder

Arrange the pork in a shallow dish. Mix together the remaining ingredients, pour over the pork, cover and marinate in the refrigerator overnight, turning and basting occasionally.

Arrange the pork slices on a rack in a roasting tin filled with a little water and baste well with the marinade. Roast in a preheated oven at 180°C/350°F/gas mark 5 for about 1 hour, basting occasionally, until the pork is cooked.

Pork with Spinach

Serves 6–8

30 ml/2 tbsp groundnut (peanut) oil
1.25 kg/3 lb loin of pork
250 ml/8 fl oz/1 cup chicken stock
15 ml/1 tbsp brown sugar
60 ml/4 tbsp soy sauce
900 g/2 lb spinach

Heat the oil and brown the pork on all sides. Pour off most of the fat. Add the stock, sugar and soy sauce, bring to the boil, cover and simmer for about 2 hours until the pork is cooked. Remove the meat from the pan and leave it to cool slightly, then slice it. Add the spinach to the pan and simmer, stirring gently, until softened. Drain the spinach and arrange on a warmed serving plate. Top with the pork slices and serve.

Deep-Fried Pork Balls

Serves 4

450 g/1 lb minced (ground) pork

1 slice ginger root, minced

15 ml/1 tbsp cornflour (cornstarch)

15 ml/1 tbsp water

2.5 ml/½ tsp salt

10 ml/2 tsp soy sauce

oil for deep-frying

Mix the pork and ginger. Mix the cornflour, water, salt and soy sauce then stir the mixture into the pork and mix well. Shape into walnut-sized balls. Heat the oil and fry the pork balls until they rise to the top of the oil. Remove from the oil and reheat. Return the pork to the pan and fry for 1 minute. Drain well.

Pork and Prawn Egg Rolls

Serves 4

30 ml/2 tbsp groundnut (peanut) oil

225 g/8 oz minced (ground) pork

225 g/8 oz prawns

100 g/4 oz Chinese leaves, shredded

100 g/4 oz bamboo shoots, cut into strips

100 g/4 oz water chestnuts, cut into strips

10 ml/2 tsp soy sauce

5 ml/1 tsp salt

5 ml/1 tsp sugar

3 spring onions (scallions), finely chopped

8 egg roll skins

oil for deep-frying

Heat the oil and fry the pork until sealed. Add the prawns and stir-fry for 1 minute. Add the Chinese leaves, bamboo shoots, water chestnuts, soy sauce, salt and sugar and stir-fry for 1 minute then cover and simmer for 5 minutes. Stir in the spring onions, turn into a colander and leave to drain.

Place a few spoonfuls of the filling mixture in the centre of each egg roll skin, fold up the bottom, fold in the sides, then roll upwards, enclosing the filling. Seal the edge with a little flour and water mixture then leave to dry for 30 minutes. Heat the oil and fry the egg rolls for about 10 minutes until crisp and golden brown. Drain well before serving.

Steamed Minced Pork

Serves 4

450 g/1 lb minced (ground) pork
5 ml/1 tsp cornflour (cornstarch)
2.5 ml/½ tsp salt
10 ml/2 tsp soy sauce

Mix the pork with the remaining ingredients and spread the mixture flat in a shallow ovenproof dish. Place in a steamer over boiling water and steam for about 30 minutes until cooked. Serve hot.

Deep-Fried Pork with Crab Meat

Serves 4

225 g/8 oz crab meat, flaked

100 g/4 oz mushrooms, chopped

100 g/4 oz bamboo shoots, chopped

5 ml/1 tsp cornflour (cornstarch)

2.5 ml/½ tsp salt

225 g/8 oz cooked pork, sliced

1 egg white, lightly beaten

oil for deep-frying

15 ml/1 tbsp chopped fresh flat-leaved parsley

Mix together the crab meat, mushrooms, bamboo shoots, most of the cornflour and the salt. Cut the meat into 5 cm/2 in squares. Make into sandwiches with the crab meat mixture. Coat in the egg white. Heat the oil and deep-fry the sandwiches a few at a time until golden brown. Drain well. Serve sprinkled with parsley.

Pork with Bean Sprouts

Serves 4

30 ml/2 tbsp groundnut (peanut) oil

2.5 ml/½ tsp salt

2 cloves garlic, crushed

450 g/1 lb bean sprouts

225 g/8 oz cooked pork, cubed

120 ml/4 fl oz/½ cup chicken stock

15 ml/1 tbsp soy sauce

15 ml/1 tbsp rice wine or dry sherry

5 ml/1 tsp sugar

15 ml/1 tbsp cornflour (cornstarch)

2.5 ml/½ tsp sesame oil

3 spring onions (scallions), chopped

Heat the oil and fry the salt and garlic until lightly browned. Add the bean sprouts and pork and stir-fry for 2 minutes. Add half the stock, bring to the boil, cover and simmer for 3 minutes. Mix the remaining stock with the rest of the ingredients, stir into the pan, return to the boil and simmer for 4 minutes, stirring. Serve sprinkled with spring onion.

Serves 6

1.25 kg/3 lb boneless rolled pork joint

30 ml/2 tbsp salt

freshly ground pepper

1 spring onion (scallion), chopped

2 cloves garlic, chopped

1 bottle dry white wine

Place the pork in a pan and add the salt, pepper, spring onion and garlic. Cover with boiling water, return to the boil, cover and simmer for 30 minutes. Remove the pork from the pan, leave to cool and dry for 6 hours or overnight in the refrigerator. Cut the pork into large pieces and place in a large screw-top jar. Cover with the wine, seal and store in the refrigerator for at least 1 week.

Steamed Leg of Pork

Serves 6–8

1 small leg of pork

90 ml/6 tbsp soy sauce

450 ml/¾ pt/2 cups water

45 ml/3 tbsp brown sugar

15 ml/1 tbsp rice wine or dry sherry

30 ml/2 tbsp groundnut (peanut) oil

3 cloves garlic, crushed

450 g/1 lb spinach

2.5 ml/½ tsp salt

30 ml/2 tbsp cornflour (cornstarch)

Pierce the pork skin all over with a pointed knife then rub in 30 ml/2 tbsp of soy sauce. Place in a heavy saucepan with the water, bring to the boil, cover and simmer for 40 minutes. Drain, reserving the liquid, and leave the pork to cool then place it in a heatproof bowl.

Mix together 15 ml/1 tbsp of sugar, the wine or sherry and 30 ml/2 tbsp of soy sauce then rub over the pork. Heat the oil and fry the garlic until lightly browned. Add the remaining sugar and soy sauce, pour the mixture over the pork and cover the bowl. Stand the bowl in a wok and fill with water to come half way up the sides. Cover and steam for about 1½ hours, topping up with boiling water as necessary. Cut the spinach into 5 cm/2 in pieces then sprinkle with salt. Bring a pan of water to the boil then pour over the spinach. Leave to stand for 2 minutes until the spinach begins to soften then drain and arrange on a warmed serving plate. Place the pork on top. Bring the pork stock to the boil. Blend the cornflour with a little water, stir it into the stock and simmer, stirring, until sauce clears and thickens. Pour over pork and serve.

Stir-Fried Roast Pork with Vegetables

Serves 4

50 g/2 oz/½ cup blanched almonds

30 ml/2 tbsp groundnut (peanut) oil

salt

100 g/4 oz mushrooms, diced

100 g/4 oz bamboo shoots, diced

1 onion, diced

2 stalks celery, diced

100 g/4 oz mangetout (snow peas), diced

4 water chestnuts, diced

1 spring onion (scallion), chopped

20 ml/4 fl oz/½ cup chicken stock

225 g/8 oz Barbecue-Roast Pork , cubed

15 ml/1 tbsp cornflour (cornstarch)

45 ml/3 tbsp water

2.5 ml/½ tsp sugar

freshly ground pepper

Toast the almonds until lightly browned. Heat the oil and salt then add the vegetables and stir-fry for 2 minutes until coated with oil. Add the stock, bring to the boil, cover and simmer for 2 minutes until the vegetables are almost cooked but still crisp.

Add the pork and heat through. Mix together the cornflour, water, sugar and pepper and stir into the sauce. Simmer, stirring, until the sauce clears and thickens.

Twice-Cooked Pork

Serves 4

45 ml/3 tbsp groundnut (peanut) oil

6 spring onions (scallions), chopped

1 clove garlic, crushed

1 slice ginger root, chopped

2.5 ml/½ tsp salt

225 g/8 oz cooked pork, cubed

15 ml/1 tbsp soy sauce

15 ml/1 tbsp rice wine or dry sherry

30 ml/2 tbsp chilli bean paste

Heat the oil and fry the spring onions, garlic, ginger and salt until lightly browned. Add the pork and stir-fry for 2 minutes. Add the soy sauce, wine or sherry and chilli bean paste and stir-fry for 3 minutes.

Pork Kidneys with Mangetout

Serves 4

4 pork kidneys, halved and cored

30 ml/2 tbsp groundnut (peanut) oil

2.5 ml/½ tsp salt

1 slice ginger root, minced

3 stalks celery, chopped

1 onion, chopped

30 ml/2 tbsp soy sauce

15 ml/1 tbsp rice wine or dry sherry

5 ml/1 tsp sugar

60 ml/4 tbsp chicken stock

225 g/8 oz mangetout (snow peas)

15 ml/1 tbsp cornflour (cornstarch)

45 ml/3 tbsp water

Parboil the kidneys for 10 minute then drain and rinse in cold water. Heat the oil and fry the salt and ginger for a few seconds. Add the kidneys and stir-fry for 30 seconds until coated with oil. Add the celery and onion and stir-fry for 2 minutes. Add the soy sauce, wine or sherry and sugar and stir-fry for 1 minute. Add the stock, bring to the boil, cover and simmer for 1 minute. Stir in the mangetout, cover and simmer for 1 minute. Mix the cornflour and water then stir it into the sauce and simmer until the sauce clears and thickens. Serve at once.

Red-Cooked Ham with Chestnuts

Serves 4–6

1.25 kg/3 lb ham

2 spring onions (scallions), halved

2 cloves garlic, crushed

45 ml/3 tbsp brown sugar

30 ml/2 tbsp rice wine or dry sherry

60 ml/4 tbsp soy sauce

450 ml/¾ pt/2 cups water

350 g/12 oz chestnuts

Place the ham in a pan with the spring onions, garlic, sugar, wine or sherry, soy sauce and water. Bring to the boil, cover and simmer for about 1½ hours, turning the ham occasionally. Blanch the chestnuts in boiling water for 5 minutes then drain. Add to the ham, cover and simmer for a further 1 hour, turning the ham once or twice.

Deep-Fried Ham and Egg Balls

Serves 4

225 g/8 oz smoked ham, minced

2 spring onions (scallions), minced

3 eggs, beaten

4 slices stale bread

10 ml/2 tbsp plain (all-purpose) flour

2.5 ml/½ tsp salt

oil for deep-frying

Mix together the ham, spring onions and eggs. Make the bread into crumbs and mix it into the ham with the flour and salt. Shape into walnut-sized balls. Heat the oil and deep-fry the meat balls until golden brown. Drain well on kitchen paper.

Ham and Pineapple

Serves 4

4 dried Chinese mushrooms

15 ml/1 tbsp groundnut (peanut) oil

1 clove garlic, crushed

50 g/2 oz water chestnuts, sliced

50 g/2 oz bamboo shoots

225 g/8 oz ham, chopped

225 g/8 oz canned pineapple chunks in fruit juice

120 ml/4 fl oz/½ cup chicken stock

15 ml/1 tbsp soy sauce

15 ml/1 tbsp cornflour (cornstarch)

Soak the mushrooms in warm water for 30 minutes then drain. Discard the stems and slice the caps. Heat the oil and fry the garlic until lightly browned. Add the mushrooms, water chestnuts and bamboo shoots and stir-fry for 2 minutes. Add the ham and drained pineapple chunks and stir-fry for 1 minute. Add 30 ml/2 tbsp of the juice from the pineapple, most of the chicken stock and the soy sauce. Bring to the boil, cover and simmer for 5 minutes. Mix the cornflour with the remaining stock and stir it into the sauce. Simmer, stirring, until the sauce clears and thickens.

Ham and Spinach Stir-Fry

Serves 4

30 ml/2 tbsp groundnut (peanut) oil

2.5 ml/½ tsp salt

1 clove garlic, minced

2 spring onions (scallions), chopped

225 g/8 oz ham, diced

450 g/1 lb spinach, shredded

60 ml/4 tbsp chicken stock

15 ml/1 tbsp cornflour (cornstarch)

15 ml/1 tbsp soy sauce

45 ml/3 tbsp water

5 ml/1 tsp sugar

Heat the oil and fry the salt, garlic and spring onions until lightly browned. Add the ham and stir-fry for 1 minute. Add the spinach and stir until coated in oil. Add the stock, bring to the boil, cover and simmer for 2 minutes until the spinach begins to wilt. Mix together the cornflour, soy sauce, water and sugar then stir it into the pan. Simmer, stirring, until the sauce thickens.

Serves 4

45 ml/3 tbsp groundnut (peanut) oil

1 clove garlic, crushed

1 spring onion (scallion), chopped

1 slice ginger root, chopped

225 g/8 oz chicken breast, cut into slivers

225 g/8 oz bamboo shoots, cut into slivers

45 ml/3 tbsp soy sauce

15 ml/1 tbsp rice wine or dry sherry

5 ml/1 tsp cornflour (cornstarch)

Heat the oil and fry the garlic, spring onion and ginger until lightly browned. Add the chicken and stir-fry for 5 minutes. Add the bamboo shoots and stir-fry for 2 minutes. Stir in the soy sauce, wine or sherry and cornflour and stir-fry for about 3 minutes until the chicken is cooked through.

Serves 6–8

900 g/2 lb fresh ham

30 ml/2 tbsp brown sugar

60 ml/4 tbsp rice wine or dry sherry

Place the ham in a heatproof dish on a rack, cover and steam over boiling water for about 1 hour. Add the sugar and wine or sherry to the dish, cover and steam for a further 1 hour or until the ham is cooked. Leave to cool in the bowl before slicing.

Serves 4

4 rashers streaky bacon, rinded and chopped

2.5 ml/½ tsp salt

1 slice ginger root, minced

½ cabbage, shredded

75 ml/5 tbsp chicken stock

15 ml/1 tbsp oyster sauce

Fry the bacon until crisp then remove it from the pan. Add the salt and ginger and stir-fry for 2 minutes. Add the cabbage and stir well then stir in the bacon and add the stock, cover and simmer for about 5 minutes until the cabbage is tender but still slightly crisp. Stir in the oyster sauce, cover and simmer for 1 minute before serving.

Almond Chicken

Serves 4–6

375 ml/13 fl oz/1½ cups chicken stock

60 ml/4 tbsp rice wine or dry sherry

45 ml/3 tbsp cornflour (cornstarch)

15 ml/1 tbsp soy sauce

4 chicken breasts

1 egg white

2.5 ml/½ tsp salt

oil for deep-frying

75 g/3 oz/½ cup blanched almonds

1 large carrot, diced

5 ml/1 tsp grated ginger root

6 spring onions (scallions), sliced

3 stalks celery, sliced

100 g/4 oz mushrooms, sliced

100 g/4 oz bamboo shoots, sliced

Mix the stock, half the wine or sherry, 30 ml/2 tbsp of cornflour, and the soy sauce in a saucepan. Bring to the boil, stirring, then simmer for 5 minutes until the mixture thickens. Remove from the heat and keep warm.

Remove the skin and bones from the chicken and cut it into 2.5 cm/1 in pieces. Mix the remaining wine or sherry and cornflour, the egg white and salt, add the chicken pieces and stir well. Heat the oil and fry the chicken pieces a few at a time for about 5 minutes until golden brown. Drain well. Remove all but 30 ml/ 2 tbsp of oil from the pan and stir-fry the almonds for 2 minutes until golden. Drain well. Add the carrot and ginger to the pan and stir-fry for 1 minute. Add the remaining vegetables and stir-fry for about 3 minutes until the vegetables are tender but still crisp. Return the chicken and almonds to the pan with the sauce and stir over a moderate heat for a few minutes until heated through.

Serves 4

6 dried Chinese mushrooms

4 chicken pieces, boned

100 g/4 oz ground almonds

salt and freshly ground pepper

60 ml/4 tbsp groundnut (peanut) oil

100 g/4 oz water chestnuts, sliced

75 ml/5 tbsp chicken stock

30 ml/2 tbsp soy sauce

Soak the mushrooms in warm water for 30 minutes then drain. Discard the stalks and slice the caps. Thinly slice the chicken. Season the almonds generously with salt and pepper and coat the chicken slices in the almonds. Heat the oil and fry the chicken until lightly browned. Add the mushrooms, water chestnuts, stock and soy sauce, bring to the boil, cover and simmer for a few minutes until the chicken is cooked.

Chicken with Almonds and Vegetables

Serves 4

75 ml/5 tbsp groundnut (peanut) oil

4 slices ginger root, minced

5 ml/1 tsp salt

100 g/4 oz Chinese cabbage, shredded

50 g/2 oz bamboo shoots, diced

50 g/2 oz mushrooms, diced

2 stalks celery, diced

3 water chestnuts, diced

120 ml/4 fl oz/½ cup chicken stock

225 g/8 oz chicken breast, diced

15 ml/1 tbsp rice wine or dry sherry

50 g/2 oz mangetout (snow peas)

100 g/4 oz flaked almonds, toasted

10 ml/2 tsp cornflour (cornstarch)

15 ml/1 tbsp water

Heat half the oil and stir-fry the ginger and salt for 30 seconds. Add the cabbage, bamboo shoots, mushrooms, celery and water chestnuts and stir-fry for 2 minutes. Add the stock, bring to the boil, cover and simmer for 2 minutes. Remove the vegetables and sauce from the pan. Heat the remaining oil and fry the chicken for 1 minute. Add the wine or sherry and fry for 1 minute. Return the vegetables to the pan with the mangetout and almonds and simmer for 30 seconds. Blend the cornflour and water to a paste, stir it into the sauce and simmer, stirring, until the sauce thickens.

Anise Chicken

Serves 4

75 ml/5 tbsp groundnut (peanut) oil

2 onions, chopped

1 clove garlic, chopped

2 slices ginger root, chopped

15 ml/1 tbsp plain (all-purpose) flour

30 ml/2 tbsp curry powder

450 g/1 lb chicken, cubed

15 ml/1 tbsp sugar

30 ml/2 tbsp soy sauce

450 ml/¾ pt/2 cups chicken stock

2 cloves star anise

225 g/8 oz potatoes, diced

Heat half the oil and fry the onions until lightly browned then remove them from the pan. Heat the remaining oil and fry the garlic and ginger for 30 seconds. Stir in the flour and curry powder and cook for 2 minutes. Return the onions to the pan, add the chicken and stir-fry for 3 minutes. Add the sugar, soy sauce, stock and anise, bring to the boil, cover and simmer for 15 minutes. Add the potatoes, return to the boil, cover and simmer for a further 20 minutes until tender.

Serves 4

4 chicken pieces

salt and freshly ground pepper

pinch of ground ginger

60 ml/4 tbsp groundnut (peanut) oil

225 g/8 oz canned apricots, halved

300 ml/½ pt/1¼ cups Sweet and Sour Sauce

30 ml/2 tbsp flaked almonds, toasted

Season the chicken with salt, pepper and ginger. Heat the oil and fry the chicken until lightly browned. Cover and cook for about 20 minutes until tender, turning occasionally. Drain off the oil. Add the apricots and sauce to the pan, bring to the boil, cover and simmer gently for about 5 minutes or until heated through. Garnish with flaked almonds.

Chicken with Asparagus

Serves 4

45 ml/3 tbsp groundnut (peanut) oil

5 ml/1 tsp salt

1 clove garlic, crushed

1 spring onion (scallion), chopped

1 chicken breast, sliced

30 ml/2 tbsp black bean sauce

350 g/12 oz asparagus, cut into 2.5 cm/1 in pieces

120 ml/4 fl oz/½ cup chicken stock

5 ml/1 tsp sugar

15 ml/1 tbsp cornflour (cornstarch)

45 ml/3 tbsp water

Heat half the oil and fry the salt, garlic and spring onion until lightly browned. Add the chicken and fry until lightly coloured. Add the black bean sauce and stir to coat the chicken. Add the asparagus, stock and sugar, bring to the boil, cover and simmer for 5 minutes until the chicken is tender. Mix the cornflour and water to a paste, stir it into the pan and simmer, stirring, until the sauce clears and thickens.

Serves 4

225 g/8 oz chicken, sliced

15 ml/1 tbsp soy sauce

15 ml/1 tbsp rice wine or dry sherry

15 ml/1 tbsp cornflour (cornstarch)

1 aubergine (eggplant), peeled and cut into strips

30 ml/2 tbsp groundnut (peanut) oil

2 dried red chilli peppers

2 cloves garlic, crushed

75 ml/5 tbsp chicken stock

Place the chicken in a bowl. Mix the soy sauce, wine or sherry and cornflour, stir into the chicken and leave to stand for 30 minutes. Blanch the aubergine in boiling water for 3 minutes then drain well. Heat the oil and fry the peppers until they darken then remove and discard them. Add the garlic and chicken and stir-fry until lightly coloured. Add the stock and aubergine, bring to the boil, cover and simmer for 3 minutes, stirring occasionally.

Bacon-Wrapped Chicken

Serves 4–6

225 g/8 oz chicken, cubed

30 ml/2 tbsp soy sauce

15 ml/1 tbsp rice wine or dry sherry

5 ml/1 tsp sugar

5 ml/1 tsp sesame oil

salt and freshly ground pepper

225 g/8 oz bacon rashers

1 eggs, lightly beaten

100 g/4 oz plain (all-purpose) flour

oil for deep-frying

4 tomatoes, sliced

Mix the chicken with the soy sauce, wine or sherry, sugar, sesame oil, salt and pepper. Cover and leave to marinate for 1 hour, stirring occasionally, then remove the chicken and discard the marinade. Cut the bacon into pieces and wrap it around the chicken cubes. Beat the eggs with the flour to make a thick batter, adding a little milk if necessary. Dip the cubes in the batter. Heat the oil and deep-fry the cubes until golden brown and cooked through. Serve garnished with tomatoes.

Chicken with Bean Sprouts

Serves 4

45 ml/3 tbsp groundnut (peanut) oil

1 clove garlic, crushed

1 spring onion (scallion), chopped

1 slice ginger root, chopped

225 g/8 oz chicken breast, cut into slivers

225 g/8 oz bean sprouts

45 ml/3 tbsp soy sauce

15 ml/1 tbsp rice wine or dry sherry

5 ml/1 tsp cornflour (cornstarch)

Heat the oil and fry the garlic, spring onion and ginger until lightly browned. Add the chicken and stir-fry for 5 minutes. Add the bean sprouts and stir-fry for 2 minutes. Stir in the soy sauce, wine or sherry and cornflour and stir-fry for about 3 minutes until the chicken is cooked through.

Serves 4

30 ml/2 tbsp groundnut (peanut) oil

5 ml/1 tsp salt

30 ml/2 tbsp black bean sauce

2 cloves garlic, crushed

450 g/1 lb chicken, diced

250 ml/8 fl oz/1 cup stock

1 green pepper, diced

1 onion, chopped

15 ml/1 tbsp soy sauce

freshly ground pepper

15 ml/1 tbsp cornflour (cornstarch)

45 ml/3 tbsp water

Heat the oil and fry the salt, black beans and garlic for 30 seconds. Add the chicken and fry until lightly browned. Stir in the stock, bring to the boil, cover and simmer for 10 minutes. Add the pepper, onion, soy sauce and pepper, cover and simmer for a further 10 minutes. Blend the cornflour and water to a paste, stir into the sauce and simmer, stirring, until the sauce thickens and the chicken is tender.

Serves 4

450 g/1 lb chicken meat, diced

225 g/8 oz chicken livers

45 ml/3 tbsp plain (all-purpose) flour

45 ml/3 tbsp groundnut (peanut) oil

1 onion, diced

1 red pepper, diced

1 green pepper, diced

225 g/8 oz broccoli florets

4 slices pineapple, diced

30 ml/2 tbsp tomato purée (paste)

30 ml/2 tbsp hoisin sauce

30 ml/2 tbsp honey

30 ml/2 tbsp soy sauce

300 ml/½ pt/1¼ cups chicken stock

10 ml/2 tsp sesame oil

Toss the chicken and chicken livers in the flour. Heat the oil and stir-fry the liver for 5 minutes then remove from the pan. Add the chicken, cover and fry over a moderate heat for 15 minutes, stirring occasionally. Add the vegetables and pineapple and stir-fry for 8 minutes. Return the livers to the wok, add the remaining ingredients and bring to the boil. Simmer, stirring, until the sauce thickens.

Chicken with Cabbage and Peanuts

Serves 4

45 ml/3 tbsp groundnut (peanut) oil
30 ml/2 tbsp peanuts
450 g/1 lb chicken, diced
½ cabbage, cut into squares
15 ml/1 tbsp black bean sauce
2 red chilli peppers, minced
5 ml/1 tsp salt

Heat a little oil and fry the peanuts for a few minutes, stirring continuously. Remove, drain then crush. Heat the remaining oil and fry the chicken and cabbage until lightly browned. Remove from the pan. Add the black bean sauce and chilli peppers and stir-fry for 2 minutes. Return the chicken and cabbage to the pan with the crushed peanuts and season with salt. Stir-fry until heated through then serve at once.

Chicken with Cashews

Serves 4

30 ml/2 tbsp soy sauce

30 ml/2 tbsp cornflour (cornstarch)

15 ml/1 tbsp rice wine or dry sherry

350 g/12 oz chicken, cubed

45 ml/3 tbsp groundnut (peanut) oil

2.5 ml/½ tsp salt

2 cloves garlic, crushed

225 g/8 oz mushrooms, sliced

100 g/4 oz water chestnuts, sliced

100 g/4 oz bamboo shoots

50 g/2 oz mangetout (snow peas)

225 g/8 oz/2 cups cashew nuts

300 ml/½ pt/1¼ cups chicken stock

Mix together the soy sauce, cornflour and wine or sherry, pour over the chicken, cover and leave to marinate for at least 1 hour. Heat 30 ml/2 tbsp of oil with the salt and garlic and fry until the garlic is lightly browned. Add the chicken with the marinade and stir-fry for 2 minutes until the chicken is lightly browned. Add the mushrooms, water chestnuts, bamboo shoots and mangetout and stir-fry for 2 minutes. Meanwhile, heat the remaining oil in a separate pan and fry the cashew nuts over a gentle heat for a few minutes until golden brown. Add them to the pan with the stock, bring to the boil, cover and simmer for 5 minutes. If the sauce has not thickened sufficiently, stir in a little cornflour blended with a spoonful of water and stir until the sauce thickens and clears.

Serves 4

225 g/8 oz chicken, sliced

5 ml/1 tsp salt

15 ml/1 tbsp soy sauce

oil for deep-frying

250 ml/8 fl oz/1 cup chicken stock

200 g/7 oz water chestnuts, chopped

225 g/8 oz chestnuts, chopped

225 g/8 oz mushrooms, quartered

15 ml/1 tbsp chopped fresh parsley

Sprinkle the chicken with salt and soy sauce and rub it well into the chicken. Heat the oil and deep-fry the chicken until golden brown then remove and drain. Place the chicken in a pan with the stock, bring to the boil and simmer for 5 minutes. Add the water chestnuts, chestnuts and mushrooms, cover and simmer for about 20 minutes until everything is tender. Serve garnished with parsley.

Serves 4

350 g/1 lb chicken meat, cubed

1 egg, lightly beaten

10 ml/2 tsp soy sauce

2.5 ml/½ tsp cornflour (cornstarch)

oil for deep-frying

1 green pepper, diced

4 cloves garlic, crushed

2 red chilli peppers, shredded

5 ml/1 tsp freshly ground pepper

5 ml/1 tsp wine vinegar

5 ml/1 tsp water

2.5 ml/½ tsp sugar

2.5 ml/½ tsp chilli oil

2.5 ml/½ tsp sesame oil

Mix the chicken with the egg, half the soy sauce and the cornflour and leave to stand for 30 minutes. Heat the oil and deep-fry the chicken until golden brown then drain well. Pour off all but 15 ml/1 tbsp of oil from the pan, add the pepper, garlic and chilli peppers and fry for 30 seconds. Add the pepper, wine vinegar, water and sugar and fry for 30 seconds. Return the chicken to the pan and stir-fry for a few minutes until cooked through. Serve sprinkled with chilli and sesame oils.

Stir-Fried Chicken with Chilli

Serves 4

225 g/8 oz chicken, sliced

2.5 ml/½ tsp soy sauce

2.5 ml/½ tsp sesame oil

2.5 ml/½ tsp rice wine or dry sherry

5 ml/1 tsp cornflour (cornstarch)

salt

45 ml/3 tbsp groundnut (peanut) oil

100 g/4 oz spinach

4 spring onions (scallions), chopped

2.5 ml/½ tsp chilli powder

15 ml/1 tbsp water

1 tomato, sliced

Mix the chicken with the soy sauce, sesame oil, wine or sherry, half the cornflour and a pinch of salt. Leave to stand for 30 minutes. Heat 15 ml/ 1 tbsp of oil and fry the chicken until lightly browned. Remove from the wok. Heat 15 ml/1 tbsp of oil and stir-fry the spinach until wilted then remove it from the wok. Heat the remaining oil and fry the spring onions, chilli powder, water and remaining cornflour for 2 minutes. Stir in the chicken and stir-fry quickly. Arrange the spinach around a warmed serving plate, top with the chicken and serve garnished with tomatoes.

Chicken Chop Suey

Serves 4

100 g/4 oz Chinese leaves, shredded

100 g/4 oz bamboo shoots, cut into strips

60 ml/4 tbsp groundnut (peanut) oil

3 spring onions (scallions), sliced

2 cloves garlic, crushed

1 slice ginger root, chopped

225 g/8 oz chicken breast, cut into strips

45 ml/3 tbsp soy sauce

15 ml/1 tbsp rice wine or dry sherry

5 ml/1 tsp salt

2.5 ml/½ tsp sugar

freshly ground pepper

15 ml/1 tbsp cornflour (cornstarch)

Blanch the Chinese leaves and bamboo shoots in boiling water for 2 minutes. Drain and pat dry. Heat 45 ml/3 tbsp of oil and fry the onions, garlic and ginger until lightly browned. Add the chicken and stir-fry for 4 minutes. Remove from the pan. Heat the remaining oil and stir-fry the vegetables for 3 minutes. Add the chicken, soy sauce, wine or sherry, salt, sugar and a pinch of pepper and stir-fry for 1 minute. Mix the cornflour with a little water, stir it into the sauce and simmer, stirring, until the sauce clears and thickens.

Chicken Chow Mein

Serves 4

30 ml/2 tbsp groundnut (peanut) oil

2 cloves garlic, crushed

450 g/1 lb chicken, sliced

225 g/8 oz bamboo shoots, sliced

100 g/4 oz celery, sliced

225 g/8 oz mushrooms, sliced

450 ml/¾ pt/2 cups chicken stock

225 g/8 oz bean sprouts

4 onions, cut into wedges

30 ml/2 tbsp soy sauce

30 ml/2 tbsp cornflour (cornstarch)

225 g/8 oz dried Chinese noodles

Heat the oil with the garlic until lightly golden then add the chicken and stir-fry for 2 minutes until lightly browned. Add the bamboo shoots, celery and mushrooms and stir-fry for 3 minutes. Add most of the stock, bring to the boil, cover and simmer for 8 minutes. Add the bean sprouts and onions and simmer for 2 minutes, stirring, until there is just a little stock remaining. Mix together the remaining stock with the soy sauce and cornflour. Stir it into the pan and simmer, stirring, until the sauce clears and thickens.

Meanwhile, cook the noodles in boiling salted water for a few minutes, according to the instructions on the packet. Drain well then toss with the chicken mixture and serve at once.

Serves 4

450 g/1 lb chicken meat, cut into chunks

30 ml/2 tbsp soy sauce

30 ml/2 tbsp plum sauce

45 ml/3 tbsp mango chutney

1 clove garlic, crushed

2.5 ml/½ tsp ground ginger

few drops of brandy

30 ml/2 tbsp cornflour (cornstarch)

2 eggs, beaten

100 g/4 oz/1 cup dried breadcrumbs

30 ml/2 tbsp groundnut (peanut) oil

6 spring onions (scallions), chopped

1 red pepper, diced

1 green pepper, diced

30 ml/2 tbsp soy sauce

30 ml/2 tbsp honey

30 ml/2 tbsp wine vinegar

Place the chicken in a bowl. Mix the sauces, chutney, garlic, ginger and brandy, pour over the chicken, cover and leave to marinate for 2 hours. Drain the chicken then dust it with cornflour. Coat in eggs then breadcrumbs. Heat the oil then fry the chicken until golden brown. Remove from the pan. Add the vegetables and stir-fry for 4 minutes then remove. Drain the oil from the pan then return the chicken and vegetables to the pan with the remaining ingredients. Bring to the boil and heat through before serving.

Fried Chicken with Cucumber

Serves 4

225 g/8 oz chicken meat

1 egg white

2.5 ml/½ tsp cornflour (cornstarch)

salt

½ cucumber

30 ml/2 tbsp groundnut (peanut) oil

100 g/4 oz button mushrooms

50 g/2 oz bamboo shoots, cut into strips

50 g/2 oz ham, diced

15 ml/1 tbsp water

2.5 ml/½ tsp salt

2.5 ml/½ tsp rice wine or dry sherry

2.5 ml/½ tsp sesame oil

Slice the chicken and cut it into chunks. Mix with the egg white, cornflour and salt and leave to stand. Halve the cucumber lengthways and cut diagonally into thick slices. Heat the oil and stir-fry the chicken until lightly browned then remove from the pan. Add the cucumber and bamboo shoots and stir-fry for 1 minute. Return the chicken to the pan with the ham, water, salt and wine or sherry. Bring to the boil and simmer until the chicken is tender. Serve sprinkled with sesame oil.

Chilli-Chicken Curry

Serves 4

120 ml/4 fl oz/½ cup groundnut (peanut) oil

4 chicken pieces

1 onion, chopped

5 ml/1 tsp curry powder

5 ml/1 tsp chilli sauce

15 ml/1 tbsp rice wine or dry sherry

2.5 ml/½ tsp salt

600 ml/1 pt/2½ cups chicken stock

15 ml/1 tbsp cornflour (cornstarch)

45 ml/3 tbsp water

5 ml/1 tsp sesame oil

Heat the oil and fry the chicken pieces until golden brown on both sides then remove them from the pan. Add the onion, curry powder and chilli sauce and stir-fry for 1 minute. Add the wine or sherry and salt, stir well, then return the chicken to the pan and stir again. Add the stock, bring to the boil and simmer gently for about 30 minutes until the chicken is tender. If the sauce has not reduced sufficiently, blend the cornflour and water to a paste, stir a little into the sauce and simmer, stirring, until the sauce thickens. Serve sprinkled with sesame oil.

Chinese Chicken Curry

Serves 4

45 ml/3 tbsp curry powder

1 onion, sliced

350 g/12 oz chicken, diced

150 ml/¼ pt/generous ½ cup chicken stock

5 ml/1 tsp salt

10 ml/2 tsp cornflour (cornstarch)

15 ml/1 tbsp water

Heat the curry powder and onion in a dry pan for 2 minutes, shaking the pan to coat the onion. Add the chicken and stir until well coated in curry powder. Add the stock and salt, bring to the boil, cover and simmer for about 5 minutes until the chicken is tender. Mix the cornflour and water to a paste, stir into the pan and simmer, stirring, until the sauce thickens.

Quick Curried Chicken

Serves 4

450 g/1 lb chicken breasts, cubed

45 ml/3 tbsp rice wine or dry sherry

50 g/2 oz cornflour (cornstarch)

1 egg white

salt

150 ml/¼ pt/generous ½ cup groundnut (peanut) oil

15 ml/1 tbsp curry powder

10 ml/2 tsp brown sugar

150 ml/¼ pt/generous ½ cup chicken stock

Mix together the chicken cubes and sherry. Reserve 10 ml/2 tsp of the cornflour. Beat the egg white with the remaining cornflour and a pinch of salt then stir it into the chicken until it is well coated. Heat the oil and fry the chicken until cooked and golden. Remove from the pan and drain off all but 15 ml/1 tbsp of the oil. Stir in the reserved cornflour, curry powder and sugar and fry for 1 minute. Stir in the stock, bring to the boil and simmer, stirring continuously, until the sauce thickens. Return the chicken to the pan, stir together and reheat before serving.

Serves 4

45 ml/3 tbsp groundnut (peanut) oil

2.5 ml/½ tsp salt

1 clove garlic, crushed

750 g/1½ lb chicken, cubed

225 g/8 oz potatoes, cubed

4 onions, cut into wedges

15 ml/1 tbsp curry powder

450 ml/¾ pt/2 cups chicken stock

225 g/8 oz mushrooms, sliced

Heat the oil with the salt and garlic, add the chicken and fry until lightly browned. Add the potatoes, onions and curry powder and stir-fry for 2 minutes. Add the stock, bring to the boil, cover and simmer for about 20 minutes until the chicken is cooked, stirring occasionally. Add the mushrooms, remove the lid and simmer for a further 10 minutes until the liquid has reduced.

Deep-Fried Chicken Legs

Serves 4

2 large chicken legs, boned

2 spring onions (scallions)

1 slice ginger, beaten flat

120 ml/4 fl oz/½ cup soy sauce

5 ml/1 tsp rice wine or dry sherry

oil for deep-frying

5 ml/1 tsp sesame oil

freshly ground pepper

Spread out the chicken flesh and score it all over. Beat 1 spring onion flat and chop the other. Mix tine flattened spring onion with the ginger, soy sauce and wine or sherry. Pour over the chicken and leave to marinate for 30 minutes. Remove and drain. Place on a plate on a steamer rack and steam for 20 minutes.

Heat the oil and deep-fry the chicken for about 5 minutes until golden brown. Remove from the pan, drain well and slice thickly, then arrange the slices on a warmed serving plate. Heat the sesame oil, add the chopped spring onion and pepper, pour over the chicken and serve.

Serves 4

1 egg, lightly beaten

30 ml/2 tbsp cornflour (cornstarch)

25 g/1 oz/¼ cup plain (all-purpose) flour

2.5 ml/½ tsp salt

225 g/8 oz chicken, cubed

oil for deep-frying

30 ml/2 tbsp groundnut (peanut) oil

30 ml/2 tbsp curry powder

60 ml/4 tbsp rice wine or dry sherry

Beat the egg with the cornflour, flour and salt to a thick batter. Pour over the chicken and stir well to coat. Heat the oil and deep-fry the chicken until golden brown and cooked through. Meanwhile, heat the oil and fry the curry powder for 1 minute. Stir in the wine or sherry and bring to the boil. Place the chicken on a warmed plate and pour over the curry sauce.

Drunken Chicken

Serves 4

450 g/1 lb chicken fillet, cut into chunks

60 ml/4 tbsp soy sauce

30 ml/2 tbsp hoisin sauce

30 ml/2 tbsp plum sauce

30 ml/2 tbsp wine vinegar

2 cloves garlic, crushed

pinch of salt

few drops of chilli oil

2 egg whites

60 ml/4 tbsp cornflour (cornstarch)

oil for deep-frying

200 ml/½ pt/1¼ cups rice wine or dry sherry

Place the chicken in a bowl. Mix the sauces and wine vinegar, garlic, salt and chilli oil, pour over the chicken and marinate in the refrigerator for 4 hours. Beat the egg whites until stiff and fold in the cornflour. Remove the chicken from the marinade and coat with the egg white mixture. Heat the oil and deep-fry the chicken until cooked through and golden brown. Drain well on kitchen paper and place in a bowl. Pour over the wine or sherry, cover and leave to marinate in the refrigerator for 12 hours. Remove the chicken from the wine and serve cold.

Savoury Chicken with Eggs

Serves 4

30 ml/2 tbsp groundnut (peanut) oil

4 chicken pieces

2 spring onions (scallions), chopped

1 clove garlic, crushed

1 slice ginger root, chopped

175 ml/6 fl oz/¾ cup soy sauce

30 ml/2 tbsp rice wine or dry sherry

30 ml/2 tbsp brown sugar

5 ml/1 tsp salt

375 ml/13 fl oz/1½ cups water

4 hard-boiled (hard-cooked) eggs

15 ml/1 tbsp cornflour (cornstarch)

Heat the oil and fry the chicken pieces until golden brown. Add the spring onions, garlic and ginger and fry for 2 minutes. Add the soy sauce, wine or sherry, sugar and salt and stir together well. Add the water and bring to the boil, cover and simmer for 20 minutes. Add the hard-boiled eggs, cover and cook for a further 15 minutes. Mix the cornflour with a little water, stir it into the sauce and simmer, stirring, until the sauce clears and thickens.

Chicken Egg Rolls

Serves 4

4 dried Chinese mushrooms

100 g/4 oz chicken, cut into strips

5 ml/1 tsp cornflour (cornstarch)

15 ml/1 tbsp soy sauce

2.5 ml/½ tsp salt

2.5 ml/½ tsp sugar

60 ml/4 tbsp groundnut (peanut) oil

225 g/8 oz bean sprouts

3 spring onions (scallions), chopped

100 g/4 oz spinach

12 egg roll skins

1 egg, beaten

oil for deep-frying

Soak the mushrooms in warm water for 30 minutes then drain. Discard the stalks and chop the caps. Place the chicken in a bowl. Mix the cornflour with 5 ml/1 tsp of soy sauce, the salt and sugar and stir into the chicken. Leave to stand for 15 minutes. Heat half the oil and stir-fry the chicken until lightly browned. Blanch the bean sprouts in boiling water for 3 minutes then drain. Heat the remaining oil and fry the spring onions until lightly browned. Stir in the mushrooms, bean sprouts, spinach and remaining soy sauce. Add in the chicken and stir-fry for 2 minutes. Leave to cool. Place a little filling on the centre of each skin and brush the edges with beaten egg. Fold in the sides then roll up the egg rolls, sealing the edges with egg. Heat the oil and deep-fry the egg rolls until crisp and golden.

Serves 4

30 ml/2 tbsp groundnut (peanut) oil

4 chicken breast fillets, cut into strips

1 red pepper, cut into strips

1 green pepper, cut into strips

45 ml/3 tbsp soy sauce

45 ml/3 tbsp rice wine or dry sherry

250 ml/8 fl oz/1 cup chicken stock

100 g/4 oz iceberg lettuce, shredded

5 ml/1 tsp brown sugar

30 ml/2 tbsp hoisin sauce

salt and pepper

15 ml/1 tbsp cornflour (cornstarch)

30 ml/2 tbsp water

4 eggs

30 ml/2 tbsp sherry

Heat the oil and fry the chicken and peppers until golden brown. Add the soy sauce, wine or sherry and stock, bring to the boil, cover and simmer for 30 minutes. Add the lettuce, sugar and hoisin sauce and season with salt and pepper. Mix the cornflour and water, stir it into the sauce and bring to the boil, stirring.

Beat the eggs with the sherry and fry as thin omelettes. Sprinkle with salt and pepper and tear into strips. Arrange in a warmed serving dish and spoon over the chicken.

Far Eastern Chicken

Serves 4

60 ml/4 tbsp groundnut (peanut) oil

450 g/1 lb chicken meat, cut into chunks

2 cloves garlic, crushed

2.5 ml/½ tsp salt

2 onions, chopped

2 pieces stem ginger, chopped

45 ml/3 tbsp soy sauce

30 ml/2 tbsp hoisin sauce

45 ml/3 tbsp rice wine or dry sherry

300 ml/½ pt/1¼ cups chicken stock

5 ml/1 tsp freshly ground pepper

6 hard-boiled (hard-cooked) eggs, chopped

15 ml/1 tbsp cornflour (cornstarch)

15 ml/1 tbsp water

Heat the oil and fry the chicken until golden brown. Add the garlic, salt, onions and ginger and fry for 2 minutes. Add the soy sauce, hoisin sauce, wine or sherry, stock and pepper. Bring to the boil, cover and simmer for 30 minutes. Add the eggs. Mix the cornflour and water and stir it into the sauce. Bring to the boil and simmer, stirring, until the sauce thickens.

Chicken Foo Yung

Serves 4

6 eggs, beaten

45 ml/3 tbsp cornflour (cornstarch)

100 g/4 oz mushrooms, roughly chopped

225 g/8 oz chicken breast, diced

1 onion, finely chopped

5 ml/1 tsp salt

45 ml/3 tbsp groundnut (peanut) oil

Beat the eggs then beat in the cornflour. Stir in all the remaining ingredients except the oil. Heat the oil. Pour the mixture into the pan a little at a time to make small pancakes about 7.5 cm/3 in across. Cook until the bottom is golden brown then turn and cook the other side.

Serves 4

6 eggs, beaten

45 ml/3 tbsp cornflour (cornstarch)

100 g/4 oz ham, diced

225 g/8 oz chicken breast, diced

3 spring onions (scallions), finely chopped

5 ml/1 tsp salt

45 ml/3 tbsp groundnut (peanut) oil

Beat the eggs then beat in the cornflour. Stir in all the remaining ingredients except the oil. Heat the oil. Pour the mixture into the pan a little at a time to make small pancakes about 7.5 cm/3 in across. Cook until the bottom is golden brown then turn and cook the other side.

Serves 4

1 chicken, halved

4 slices ginger root, crushed

30 ml/2 tbsp rice wine or dry sherry

30 ml/2 tbsp soy sauce

5 ml/1 tsp sugar

oil for deep-frying

Place the chicken in a shallow bowl. Mix the ginger, wine or sherry, soy sauce and sugar, pour over the chicken and rub into the skin. Leave to marinate for 1 hour. Heat the oil and deep-fry the chicken, one half at a time, until lightly coloured. Remove from the oil and leave to cool slightly while you reheat the oil. Return the chicken to the pan and deep-fry until golden brown and cooked through. Drain well before serving.

Ginger Chicken

Serves 4

225 g/8 oz chicken, thinly sliced

1 egg white

pinch of salt

2.5 ml/½ tsp cornflour (cornstarch)

15 ml/1 tbsp groundnut (peanut) oil

10 slices ginger root

6 mushrooms, halved

1 carrot, sliced

2 spring onions (scallions), sliced

5 ml/1 tsp rice wine or dry sherry

5 ml/1 tsp water

2.5 ml/½ tsp sesame oil

Mix the chicken with the egg white, salt and cornflour. Heat half the oil and fry the chicken until lightly browned then remove it from the pan. Heat the remaining oil and fry the ginger, mushrooms, carrot and spring onions for 3 minutes. Return the chicken to the pan with the wine or sherry and water and simmer until the chicken is tender. Serve sprinkled with sesame oil.

Serves 4

60 ml/4 tbsp groundnut (peanut) oil

225 g/8 oz onions, sliced

450 g/1 lb chicken meat, diced

100 g/4 oz mushrooms, sliced

30 ml/2 tbsp plain (all-purpose) flour

60 ml/4 tbsp soy sauce

10 ml/2 tsp sugar

salt and freshly ground pepper

900 ml/1½ pt/3¾ cups hot water

2 slices ginger root, chopped

450 g/1 lb water chestnuts

Heat the half oil and fry the onions for 3 minutes then remove them from the pan. Heat the remaining oil and fry the chicken until lightly browned.

Add the mushrooms and cook for 2 minutes. Sprinkle the mixture with flour then stir in the soy sauce, sugar, salt and pepper. Pour in the water and ginger, onions and chestnuts. Bring to the boil, cover and simmer gently for 20 minutes. Remove the lid and continue to simmer gently until the sauce has reduced.

Serves 4

8 small chicken pieces

300 ml/½ pt/1¼ cups chicken stock

45 ml/3 tbsp soy sauce

15 ml/1 tbsp rice wine or dry sherry

5 ml/1 tsp sugar

1 sliced ginger root, minced

Place all the ingredients in a large pan, bring to the boil, cover and simmer for about 30 minutes until the chicken is thoroughly cooked. Remove the lid and continue to simmer until the sauce has reduced.

Serves 4

4 chicken pieces

300 ml/½ pt/1¼ cups soy sauce

oil for deep-frying

4 spring onions (scallions), thickly sliced

1 slice ginger root, minced

2 red chilli peppers, sliced

3 cloves star anise

50 g/2 oz bamboo shoots, sliced

150 ml/1½ pt/generous ½ cup chicken stock

30 ml/2 tbsp cornflour (cornstarch)

60 ml/4 tbsp water

5 ml/1 tsp sesame oil

Cut the chicken into large chunks and marinate in the soy sauce for 10 minutes. Remove and drain, reserving the soy sauce. Heat the oil and deep-fry the chicken for about 2 minutes until lightly browned. Remove and drain. Pour off all but 30 ml/2 tbsp of the oil then add the spring onions, ginger, chilli peppers and star anise and fry for 1 minute. Return the chicken to the pan with the bamboo shoots and reserved soy sauce and add just enough stock to cover the chicken. Bring to the boil and simmer for about 10 minutes until the chicken is tender. Remove the chicken from the sauce with a slotted spoon and arrange on a warmed serving dish. Strain the sauce then return it to the pan. Blend the cornflour and water to a paste, stir into the sauce and simmer, stirring, until the sauce thickens. Pour over the chicken and serve sprinkled with a little sesame oil.

Golden Coins

Serves 4

4 chicken breast fillets

30 ml/2 tbsp honey

30 ml/2 tbsp wine vinegar

30 ml/2 tbsp tomato ketchup (catsup)

30 ml/2 tbsp soy sauce

pinch of salt

2 cloves garlic, crushed

5 ml/1 tsp five-spice powder

45 ml/3 tbsp plain (all-purpose) flour

2 eggs, beaten

5 ml/1 tsp grated root ginger

5 ml/1 tsp grated lemon rind

100 g/4 oz/1 cup dried breadcrumbs

oil for deep-frying

Put the chicken into a bowl. Mix together the honey, wine vinegar, tomato ketchup, soy sauce, salt, garlic and five-spice powder. Pour over the chicken, stir well, cover and marinate in the refrigerator for 12 hours.

Remove the chicken from the marinade and cut into finger thick strips. Dust with flour. Beat the eggs, ginger and lemon rind.

Coat the chicken in the mixture then in the breadcrumbs until evenly coated. Heat the oil and deep-fry the chicken until golden brown.

Steamed Chicken with Ham

Serves 4

4 chicken portions
100 g/4 oz smoked ham, chopped
3 spring onions (scallions), chopped
15 ml/1 tbsp groundnut (peanut) oil
salt and freshly ground pepper
15 ml/1 tbsp flat-leaved parsley

Chop the chicken portions into 5 cm/1 in chunks and place in an ovenproof bowl with the ham and spring onions. Sprinkle with oil and season with salt and pepper then toss the ingredients together gently. Place the bowl on a rack in a steamer, cover and steam over boiling water for about 40 minutes until the chicken is tender. Serve garnished with parsley.

Chicken with Hoisin Sauce

Serves 4

4 chicken portions, halved

50 g/2 oz/½ cup cornflour (cornstarch)

oil for deep-frying

10 ml/2 tsp grated ginger root

2 onions, chopped

225 g/8 oz broccoli florets

1 red pepper, chopped

225 g/8 oz button mushrooms

250 ml/8 fl oz/1 cup chicken stock

45 ml/3 tbsp rice wine or dry sherry

45 ml/3 tbsp cider vinegar

45 ml/3 tbsp hoisin sauce

20 ml/4 tsp soy sauce

Coat the chicken pieces in half the cornflour. Heat the oil and fry the chicken pieces a few at a time for about 8 minutes until golden brown and cooked through. Remove from the pan and drain on kitchen paper. Remove all but 30 ml/2 tbsp of oil from the pan and stir-fry the ginger for 1 minute. Add the onions and stir-fry for 1 minute. Add the broccoli, pepper and mushrooms and stir-fry for 2 minutes. Combine the stock with the reserved cornflour and remaining ingredients and add to the pan. Bring to the boil, stirring, and cook until the sauce clears. Return the chicken to the wok and cook, stirring, for about 3 minutes until heated through.

Honey Chicken

Serves 4

30 ml/2 tbsp groundnut (peanut) oil

4 chicken pieces

30 ml/2 tbsp soy sauce

120 ml/4 fl oz/½ cup rice wine or dry sherry

30 ml/2 tbsp honey

5 ml/1 tsp salt

1 spring onion (scallion), chopped

1 slice ginger root, finely chopped

Heat the oil and fry the chicken until browned on all sides. Drain off excess oil. Mix together the remaining ingredients and pour them into the pan. Bring to the boil, cover and simmer for about 40 minutes until the chicken is cooked through.

Kung Pao Chicken

Serves 4

450 g/1 lb chicken, cubed

1 egg white

5 ml/1 tsp salt

30 ml/2 tbsp cornflour (cornstarch)

60 ml/4 tbsp groundnut (peanut) oil

25 g/1 oz dried red chilli peppers, trimmed

5 ml/1 tsp minced garlic

15 ml/1 tbsp soy sauce

15 ml/1 tbsp rice wine or dry sherry 5 ml/1 tsp sugar

5 ml/1 tsp wine vinegar

5 ml/1 tsp sesame oil

30 ml/2 tbsp water

Place the chicken in a bowl with the egg white, salt and half the cornflour and leave to marinate for 30 minutes. Heat the oil and fry the chicken until lightly browned then remove it from the pan. Reheat the oil and fry the chilli peppers and garlic for 2 minutes. Return the chicken to the pan with the soy sauce, wine or sherry, sugar, wine vinegar and sesame oil and stir-fry for 2 minutes. Mix the remaining cornflour with the water, stir it into the pan and simmer, stirring, until the sauce clears and thickens.

Serves 4

30 ml/2 tbsp groundnut (peanut) oil

5 ml/1 tsp salt

225 g/8 oz leeks, sliced

1 slice ginger root, chopped

225 g/8 oz chicken, thinly sliced

15 ml/1 tbsp rice wine or dry sherry

15 ml/1 tbsp soy sauce

Heat half the oil and fry the salt and leeks until lightly browned then remove them from the pan. Heat the remaining oil and fry the ginger and chicken until lightly browned. Add the wine or sherry and soy sauce and fry for a further 2 minutes until the chicken is cooked. Return the leeks to the pan and stir together until heated through. Serve at once.

Lemon Chicken

Serves 4

4 boned chicken breasts

2 eggs

50 g/2 oz/½ cup cornflour (cornstarch)

50 g/2 oz/½ cup plain (all-purpose) flour

150 ml/¼ pt/generous ½ cup water

groundnut (peanut) oil for deep-frying

250 ml/8 fl oz/1 cup chicken stock

60 ml/5 tbsp lemon juice

30 ml/2 tbsp rice wine or dry sherry

30 ml/2 tbsp cornflour (cornstarch)

30 ml/2 tbsp tomato purée (paste)

1 head lettuce

Cut each chicken breast into 4 pieces. Beat the eggs, cornflour and plain flour, adding just enough water to make a thick batter. Place the chicken pieces in the batter and stir until thoroughly coated. Heat the oil and deep-fry the chicken until golden brown and cooked through.

Meanwhile, mix the stock, lemon juice, wine or sherry, cornflour and tomato purée and heat gently, stirring, until the mixture comes to the boil. Simmer gently, stirring continuously, until the sauce thickens and clears. Arrange the chicken on a warmed serving plate on a bed of lettuce leaves and either pour over the sauce or serve it separately.

Lemon Chicken Stir-Fry

Serves 4

450 g/1 lb boned chicken, sliced

30 ml/2 tbsp lemon juice

15 ml/1 tbsp soy sauce

15 ml/1 tbsp rice wine or dry sherry

30 ml/2 tbsp cornflour (cornstarch)

30 ml/2 tbsp groundnut (peanut) oil

2.5 ml/½ tsp salt

2 cloves garlic, crushed

50 g/2 oz water chestnuts, cut into strips

50 g/2 oz bamboo shoots, cut into strips

a few Chinese leaves, cut into strips

60 ml/4 tbsp chicken stock

15 ml/1 tbsp tomato purée (paste)

15 ml/1 tbsp sugar

15 ml/1 tbsp lemon juice

Place the chicken in a bowl. Mix together the lemon juice, soy sauce, wine or sherry and 15 ml/1 tbsp cornflour, pour over the chicken and leave to marinate for 1 hour, turning occasionally.

Heat the oil, salt and garlic until the garlic is lightly browned then add the chicken and marinade and stir-fry for about 5 minutes until the chicken is lightly browned. Add the water chestnuts, bamboo shoots and Chinese leaves and stir-fry for a further 3 minutes or until the chicken is just cooked. Add the remaining ingredients and stir-fry for about 3 minutes until the sauce clears and thickens.

Chicken Livers with Bamboo Shoots

Serves 4

225 g/8 oz chicken livers, thickly sliced

45 ml/3 tbsp rice wine or dry sherry

45 ml/3 tbsp groundnut (peanut) oil

15 ml/1 tbsp soy sauce

100 g/4 oz bamboo shoots, sliced

100 g/4 oz water chestnuts, sliced

60 ml/4 tbsp chicken stock

salt and freshly ground pepper

Mix the chicken livers with the wine or sherry and leave to stand for 30 minutes. Heat the oil and fry the chicken livers until lightly browned. Add the marinade, soy sauce, bamboo shoots, water chestnuts and stock. Bring to the boil and season with salt and pepper. Cover and simmer for about 10 minutes until tender.

Serves 4

450 g/1 lb chicken livers, halved
50 g/2 oz/½ cup cornflour (cornstarch)
oil for deep-frying

Pat the chicken livers dry then dust with cornflour, shaking off any excess. Heat the oil and deep-fry the chicken livers for a few minutes until golden brown and cooked through. Drain on kitchen paper before serving.

Serves 4

225 g/8 oz chicken livers, thickly sliced

10 ml/2 tsp cornflour (cornstarch)

10 ml/2 tsp rice wine or dry sherry

15 ml/1 tbsp soy sauce

45 ml/3 tbsp groundnut (peanut) oil

2.5 ml/½ tsp salt

2 slices ginger root, minced

100 g/4 oz mangetout (snow peas)

10 ml/2 tsp cornflour (cornstarch)

60 ml/4 tbsp water

Place the chicken livers in a bowl. Add the cornflour, wine or sherry and soy sauce and toss well to coat. Heat half the oil and fry the salt and ginger until lightly browned. Add the mangetout and stir-fry until well coated with oil then remove from the pan. Heat the remaining oil and fry the chicken livers for 5 minutes until cooked through. Mix the cornflour and water to a paste, stir it into the pan and simmer, stirring, until the sauce clears and thickens. Return the mangetout to the pan and simmer until heated through.

Serves 4

30 ml/2 tbsp groundnut (peanut) oil

1 onion, sliced

450 g/1 lb chicken livers, halved

2 stalks celery, sliced

120 ml/4 fl oz/½ cup chicken stock

15 ml/1 tbsp cornflour (cornstarch)

15 ml/1 tbsp soy sauce

30 ml/2 tbsp water

noodle pancake

Heat the oil and fry the onion until softened. Add the chicken livers and stir-fry until coloured. Add the celery and stir-fry for 1 minute. Add the stock, bring to the boil, cover and simmer for 5 minutes. Mix the cornflour, soy sauce and water to a paste, stir it into the pan and simmer, stirring, until the sauce clears and thickens. Pour the mixture over the noodle pancake and serve.

Serves 4

45 ml/3 tbsp groundnut (peanut) oil

1 onion, chopped

225 g/8 oz chicken livers, halved

100 g/4 oz mushrooms, sliced

30 ml/2 tbsp oyster sauce

15 ml/1 tbsp soy sauce

15 ml/1 tbsp rice wine or dry sherry

120 ml/4 fl oz/½ cup chicken stock

5 ml/1 tsp sugar

15 ml/1 tbsp cornflour (cornstarch)

45 ml/3 tbsp water

Heat half the oil and fry the onion until softened. Add the chicken livers and fry until just coloured. Add the mushrooms and fry for 2 minutes. Mix the oyster sauce, soy sauce, wine or sherry, stock and sugar, pour it into the pan and bring to the boil, stirring. Mix the cornflour and water to a paste, add it to the pan and simmer, stirring until the sauce clears and thickens and the livers are tender.

Serves 4

225 g/8 oz chicken livers, halved

45 ml/3 tbsp groundnut (peanut) oil

30 ml/2 tbsp soy sauce

15 ml/1 tbsp cornflour (cornstarch)

15 ml/1 tbsp sugar

15 ml/1 tbsp wine vinegar

salt and freshly ground pepper

100 g/4 oz pineapple chunks

60 ml/4 tbsp chicken stock

Blanch the chicken livers in boiling water for 30 seconds then drain. Heat the oil and stir-fry the chicken livers for 30 seconds. Mix together the soy sauce, cornflour, sugar, wine vinegar, salt and pepper, pour into the pan and stir well to coat the chicken livers. Add the pineapple chunks and stock and stir-fry for about 3 minutes until the livers are cooked.

Serves 4

30 ml/2 tbsp groundnut (peanut) oil

450 g/1 lb chicken livers, quartered

2 green peppers, cut into chunks

4 slices canned pineapple, cut into chunks

60 ml/4 tbsp chicken stock

30 ml/2 tbsp cornflour (cornstarch)

10 ml/2 tsp soy sauce

100 g/4 oz/½ cup sugar

120 ml/4 fl oz/½ cup wine vinegar

120 ml/4 fl oz/½ cup water

Heat the oil and fry the livers until lightly browned then transfer them to a warmed serving dish. Add the peppers to the pan and fry for 3 minutes. Add the pineapple and stock, bring to the boil, cover and simmer for 15 minutes. Blend the remaining ingredients to a paste, stir into the pan and simmer, stirring, until the sauce thickens. Pour over the chicken livers and serve.

Serves 4

3 chicken breasts

60 ml/4 tbsp cornflour (cornstarch)

45 ml/3 tbsp groundnut (peanut) oil

5 spring onions (scallions), sliced

1 red pepper, cut into chunks

120 ml/4 fl oz/½ cup tomato sauce

120 ml/4 fl oz/½ cup chicken stock

5 ml/1 tsp sugar

275 g/10 oz peeled lychees

Cut the chicken breasts in half and remove and discard the bones and skin. Cut each breast into 6. Reserve 5 ml/1 tsp of cornflour and toss the chicken in the remainder until it is well coated. Heat the oil and stir-fry the chicken for about 8 minutes until golden brown. Add the spring onions and pepper and stir-fry for 1 minute. Mix together the tomato sauce, half the stock and the sugar and stir it into the wok with the lychees. Bring to the boil, cover and simmer for about 10 minutes until the chicken is cooked through. Mix the reserved cornflour and stock then stir it into the pan. Simmer, stirring, until the sauce clears and thickens.

Chicken with Lychee Sauce

Serves 4

225 g/8 oz chicken

1 spring onion (scallion)

4 water chestnuts

30 ml/2 tbsp cornflour (cornstarch)

45 ml/3 tbsp soy sauce

30 ml/2 tbsp rice wine or dry sherry

2 egg whites

oil for deep-frying

400 g/14 oz canned lychees in syrup

5 tbsp chicken stock

Mince (grind) the chicken with the spring onion and water chestnuts. Mix in half the cornflour, 30 ml/2 tbsp of soy sauce, the wine or sherry and the egg whites. Shape the mixture into walnut-sized balls. Heat the oil and deep-fry the chicken until golden brown. Drain on kitchen paper.

Meanwhile, heat the lychee syrup gently with the stock and reserved soy sauce. Mix the remaining cornflour with a little water, stir it into the pan and simmer, stirring, until the sauce clears and thickens. Stir in the lychees and simmer gently to heat

through. Arrange the chicken on a warmed serving plate, pour
over the lychees and sauce and serve at once.

Chicken with Mangetout

Serves 4

225 g/8 oz chicken, thinly sliced

5 ml/1 tsp cornflour (cornstarch)

5 ml/1 tsp rice wine or dry sherry

5 ml/1 tsp sesame oil

1 egg white, lightly beaten

45 ml/3 tbsp groundnut (peanut) oil

1 clove garlic, crushed

1 slice ginger root, minced

100 g/4 oz mangetout (snow peas)

120 ml/4 fl oz/½ cup chicken stock

salt and freshly ground pepper

Mix the chicken with the cornflour, wine or sherry, sesame oil
and egg white. Heat half the oil and fry the garlic and ginger until
lightly browned. Add the chicken and fry until golden then
remove from the pan. Heat the remaining oil and fry the
mangetout for 2 minutes. Add the stock, bring to the boil, cover
and simmer for 2 minutes. Return the chicken to the pan and
season with salt and pepper. Simmer gently until heated through.

Serves 4

100 g/4 oz/1 cup plain (all-purpose) flour

250 ml/8 fl oz/1 cup water

2.5 ml/½ tsp salt

pinch of baking powder

3 chicken breasts

oil for deep-frying

1 slice ginger root, minced

150 ml/¼ pt/generous ½ cup chicken stock

45 ml/3 tbsp wine vinegar

45 ml/3 tbsp rice wine or dry sherry

20 ml/4 tsp soy sauce

10 ml/2 tsp sugar

10 ml/2 tsp cornflour (cornstarch)

5 ml/1 tsp sesame oil

5 spring onions (scallions), sliced

400 g/11 oz canned mangoes, drained and cut into strips

Whisk together the flour, water, salt and baking powder. Leave to stand for 15 minutes. Remove and discard the skin and bones from the chicken. Cut the chicken into thin strips. Mix these into the flour mixture. Heat the oil and fry the chicken for about 5 minutes until golden brown. Remove from the pan and drain on kitchen paper. Remove all but 15 ml/1 tbsp of oil from the wok and stir-fry the ginger until lightly browned. Mix the stock with the wine vinegar, wine or sherry, soy sauce, sugar, cornflour and sesame oil. Add to the pan and bring to the boil, stirring. Add the spring onions and simmer for 3 minutes. Add the chicken and mangoes and simmer, stirring, for 2 minutes.

Chicken-Stuffed Melon

Serves 4

350 g/12 oz chicken meat

6 water chestnuts

2 shelled scallops

4 slices ginger root

5 ml/1 tsp salt

15 ml/1 tbsp soy sauce

600 ml/1 pt/2½ cups chicken stock

8 small or 4 medium cantaloupe melons

Finely chop the chicken, chestnuts, scallops and ginger and mix with the salt, soy sauce and stock. Cut the tops off the melons and scoop out the seeds. Serrate the top edges. Fill the melons with the chicken mixture and stand on a rack in a steamer. Steam over boiling water for 40 minutes until the chicken is cooked.

Serves 4

45 ml/3 tbsp groundnut (peanut) oil

1 clove garlic, crushed

1 spring onion (scallion), chopped

1 slice ginger root, minced

225 g/8 oz chicken breast, cut into slivers

225 g/8 oz button mushrooms

45 ml/3 tbsp soy sauce

15 ml/1 tbsp rice wine or dry sherry

5 ml/1 tsp cornflour (cornstarch)

Heat the oil and fry the garlic, spring onion and ginger until lightly browned. Add the chicken and stir-fry for 5 minutes. Add the mushrooms and stir-fry for 3 minutes. Add the soy sauce, wine or sherry and cornflour and stir-fry for about 5 minutes until the chicken is cooked through.

Serves 4

30 ml/2 tbsp groundnut (peanut) oil

2 cloves garlic, crushed

1 slice ginger root, minced

450 g/1 lb boned chicken, cubed

225 g/8 oz button mushrooms

100 g/4 oz bamboo shoots, cut into strips

1 green pepper, cubed

1 red pepper, cubed

250 ml/8 fl oz/1 cup chicken stock

30 ml/2 tbsp rice wine or dry sherry

15 ml/1 tbsp soy sauce

15 ml/1 tbsp tabasco sauce

30 ml/2 tbsp cornflour (cornstarch)

30 ml/2 tbsp water

Heat the oil, garlic and ginger until the garlic is lightly golden. Add the chicken and stir-fry until it is lightly browned. Add the mushrooms, bamboo shoots and peppers and stir-fry for 3 minutes. Add the stock, wine or sherry, soy sauce and tabasco sauce and bring to the boil, stirring. Cover and simmer for about 10 minutes until the chicken is thoroughly cooked. Mix together the cornflour and water and stir them into the sauce. Simmer, stirring, until the sauce clears and thickens, adding a little more stock or water if the sauce is too thick.

Stir-Fried Chicken with Mushrooms

Serves 4

6 dried Chinese mushrooms

1 chicken breast, thinly sliced

1 slice ginger root, minced

2 spring onions (scallions), minced

15 ml/1 tbsp cornflour (cornstarch)

15 ml/1 tbsp rice wine or dry sherry

30 ml/2 tbsp water

2.5 ml/½ tsp salt

45 ml/3 tbsp groundnut (peanut) oil

225 g/8 oz mushrooms, sliced

100 g/4 oz bean sprouts

15 ml/1 tbsp soy sauce

5 ml/1 tsp sugar

120 ml/4 fl oz/½ cup chicken stock

Soak the mushrooms in warm water for 30 minutes then drain. Discard the stalks and slice the caps. Place the chicken in a bowl. Mix the ginger, spring onions, cornflour, wine or sherry, water and salt, stir into the chicken and leave to stand for 1 hour. Heat half the oil and stir-fry the chicken until lightly browned then remove it from the pan. Heat the remaining oil and stir-fry the dried and fresh mushrooms and the bean sprouts for 3 minutes. Add the soy sauce, sugar and stock, bring to the boil, cover and simmer for 4 minutes until the vegetables are just tender. Return the chicken to the pan, stir well and reheat gently before serving.

Steamed Chicken with Mushrooms

Serves 4

4 chicken pieces
30 ml/2 tbsp cornflour (cornstarch)
30 ml/2 tbsp soy sauce
3 spring onions (scallions), chopped
2 slices root ginger, chopped
2.5 ml/½ tsp salt
100 g/4 oz mushrooms, sliced

Chop the chicken pieces into 5 cm/2 in chunks and place them in an ovenproof bowl. Mix the cornflour and soy sauce to a paste, stir in the spring onions, ginger and salt and mix well with the chicken. Gently stir in the mushrooms. Place the bowl on a rack in a steamer, cover and steam over boiling water for about 35 minutes until the chicken is tender.

Serves 4

60 ml/4 tbsp groundnut (peanut) oil

2 onions, chopped

450 g/1 lb chicken, sliced

30 ml/2 tbsp rice wine or dry sherry

250 ml/8 fl oz/1 cup chicken stock

45 ml/3 tbsp soy sauce

30 ml/2 tbsp cornflour (cornstarch)

45 ml/3 tbsp water

Heat the oil and fry the onions until lightly browned. Add the chicken and fry until lightly browned. Add the wine or sherry, stock and soy sauce, bring to the boil, cover and simmer for 25 minutes until the chicken is tender. Blend the cornflour and water to a paste, stir it into the pan and simmer, stirring, until the sauce clears and thickens.

Orange and Lemon Chicken

Serves 4

350 g/1 lb chicken meat, cut into strips

30 ml/2 tbsp groundnut (peanut) oil

2 cloves garlic, crushed

2 slices ginger root, minced

grated rind of ½ orange

grated rind of ½ lemon

45 ml/3 tbsp orange juice

45 ml/3 tbsp lemon juice

15 ml/1 tbsp soy sauce

3 spring onions (scallions), chopped

15 ml/1 tbsp cornflour (cornstarch)

45 ml/1 tbsp water

Blanch the chicken in boiling water for 30 seconds then drain. Heat the oil and stir-fry the garlic and ginger for 30 seconds. Add the orange and lemon rind and juice, soy sauce and spring onions and stir-fry for 2 minutes. Add the chicken and simmer for a few minutes until the chicken is tender. Blend the cornflour and water to a paste, stir into the pan and simmer, stirring, until the sauce thickens.

Serves 4

30 ml/2 tbsp groundnut (peanut) oil

1 clove garlic, crushed

1 slice ginger, finely chopped

450 g/1 lb chicken, sliced

250 ml/8 fl oz/1 cup chicken stock

30 ml/2 tbsp oyster sauce

15 ml/1 tbsp rice wine or sherry

5 ml/1 tsp sugar

Heat the oil with the garlic and ginger and fry until lightly browned. Add the chicken and stir-fry for about 3 minutes until lightly browned. Add the stock, oyster sauce, wine or sherry and sugar, bring to the boil, stirring, then cover and simmer for about 15 minutes, stirring occasionally, until the chicken is cooked through. Remove the lid and continue to cook, stirring, for about 4 minutes until the sauce has reduced and thickened.

Chicken Parcels

Serves 4

225 g/8 oz chicken
30 ml/2 tbsp rice wine or dry sherry
30 ml/2 tbsp soy sauce
waxed paper or baking parchment
30 ml/2 tbsp groundnut (peanut) oil
oil for deep-frying

Cut the chicken into 5 cm/2 in cubes. Mix the wine or sherry and soy sauce, pour over the chicken and stir well. Cover and leave to stand for 1 hour, stirring occasionally. Cut the paper into 10 cm/4 in squares and brush with oil. Drain the chicken well. Place a piece of paper on the work surface with one corner pointing towards you. Place a piece of chicken on the square just below the centre, fold up the bottom corner and fold up again to encase the chicken. Fold in the sides then fold down the top corner to secure the parcel. Heat the oil and deep-fry the chicken parcels for about 5 minutes until cooked. Serve hot in the parcels for the guests to open themselves.

Chicken with Peanuts

Serves 4

225 g/8 oz chicken, thinly sliced

1 egg white, lightly beaten

10 ml/2 tsp cornflour (cornstarch)

45 ml/3 tbsp groundnut (peanut) oil

1 clove garlic, crushed

1 slice ginger root, minced

2 leeks, chopped

30 ml/2 tbsp soy sauce

15 ml/1 tbsp rice wine or dry sherry

100 g/4 oz roasted peanuts

Mix the chicken with the egg white and cornflour until well coated. Heat half the oil and stir-fry the chicken until golden brown then remove from the pan. Heat the remaining oil and fry and garlic and ginger until softened. Add the leeks and fry until lightly browned. Stir in the soy sauce and wine or sherry and simmer for 3 minutes. Return the chicken to the pan with the peanuts and simmer gently until heated through.

Serves 4

4 chicken breasts, diced

salt and freshly ground pepper

5 ml/1 tsp five-spice powder

45 ml/3 tbsp groundnut (peanut) oil

1 onion, diced

2 carrots, diced

1 stick celery, diced

300 ml/½ pt/1¼ cups chicken stock

10 ml/2 tsp tomato purée (paste)

100 g/4 oz peanut butter

15 ml/1 tbsp soy sauce

10 ml/2 tsp cornflour (cornstarch)

pinch of brown sugar

15 ml/1 tbsp chopped chives

Season the chicken with salt, pepper and five-spice powder. Heat the oil and stir-fry the chicken until tender. Remove from the pan. Add the vegetables and fry until tender but still crisp. Mix the stock with the remaining ingredients except the chives, stir into the pan and bring to the boil. Return the chicken to the pan and reheat, stirring. Serve sprinkled with sugar.

Chicken with Peas

Serves 4

60 ml/4 tbsp groundnut (peanut) oil

1 onion, chopped

450 g/1 lb chicken, diced

salt and freshly ground pepper

100 g/4 oz peas

2 stalks celery, chopped

100 g/4 oz mushrooms, chopped

250 ml/8 fl oz/1 cup chicken stock

15 ml/1 tbsp cornflour (cornstarch)

15 ml/1 tbsp soy sauce

60 ml/4 tbsp water

Heat the oil and fry the onion until lightly browned. Add the chicken and fry until coloured. Season with salt and pepper and add the peas, celery and mushrooms and stir well. Add the stock, bring to the boil, cover and simmer for 15 minutes. Blend the cornflour, soy sauce and water to a paste, stir it into the pan and simmer, stirring, until the sauce clears and thickens.

Serves 4

4 chicken portions

salt and freshly ground pepper

5 ml/1 tsp sugar

1 spring onion (scallion), chopped

1 slice ginger root, minced

15 ml/1 tbsp soy sauce

15 ml/1 tbsp rice wine or dry sherry

15 ml/1 tbsp cornflour (cornstarch)

oil for deep-frying

Place the chicken portions in a shallow bowl and sprinkle with salt and pepper. Mix the sugar, spring onion, ginger, soy sauce and wine or sherry, rub into the chicken, cover and leave to marinate for 3 hours. Drain the chicken and dust it with cornflour. Heat the oil and deep-fry the chicken until golden brown and cooked through. Drain well before serving.

Chicken with Peppers

Serves 4

60 ml/4 tbsp soy sauce

45 ml/3 tbsp rice wine or dry sherry

45 ml/3 tbsp cornflour (cornstarch)

450 g/1 lb chicken, minced (ground)

60 ml/4 tbsp groundnut (peanut) oil

2.5 ml/½ tsp salt

2 cloves garlic, crushed

2 red peppers, cubed

1 green pepper, cubed

5 ml/1 tsp sugar

300 ml/½ pt/1¼ cups chicken stock

Mix together half the soy sauce, half the wine or sherry and half the cornflour. Pour over the chicken, stir well, and leave to marinate for at least 1 hour. Heat half the oil with the salt and garlic until the garlic is lightly browned. Add the chicken and marinade and stir-fry for about 4 minutes until the chicken turns white then remove from the pan. Add the remaining oil to the pan and stir-fry the peppers for 2 minutes. Add the sugar to the pan with the remaining soy sauce, wine or sherry and cornflour and mix well. Add the stock, bring to the boil then simmer, stirring, until the sauce thickens. Return the chicken to the pan, cover and simmer for 4 minutes until the chicken is cooked through.

Stir-Fried Chicken with Peppers

Serves 4

1 chicken breast, thinly sliced

2 slices ginger root, minced

2 spring onions (scallions), minced

15 ml/1 tbsp cornflour (cornstarch)

30 ml/2 tbsp rice wine or dry sherry

30 ml/2 tbsp water

2.5 ml/½ tsp salt

45 ml/3 tbsp groundnut (peanut) oil

100 g/4 oz water chestnuts, sliced

1 red pepper, cut into strips

1 green pepper, cut into strips

1 yellow pepper, cut into strips

30 ml/2 tbsp soy sauce

120 ml/4 fl oz/½ cup chicken stock

Place the chicken in a bowl. Mix the ginger, spring onions, cornflour, wine or sherry, water and salt, stir into the chicken and leave to stand for 1 hour. Heat half the oil and stir-fry the chicken until lightly browned then remove it from the pan. Heat the remaining oil and stir-fry the water chestnuts and peppers for 2 minutes. Add the soy sauce and stock, bring to the boil, cover and simmer for 5 minutes until the vegetables are just tender. Return the chicken to the pan, stir well and reheat gently before serving.

Serves 4

30 ml/2 tbsp groundnut (peanut) oil

5 ml/1 tsp salt

2 cloves garlic, crushed

450 g/1 lb boned chicken, thinly sliced

2 onions, sliced

100 g/4 oz water chestnuts, sliced

100 g/4 oz pineapple chunks

30 ml/2 tbsp rice wine or dry sherry

450 ml/¾ pt/2 cups chicken stock

5 ml/1 tsp sugar

freshly ground pepper

30 ml/2 tbsp pineapple juice

30 ml/2 tbsp soy sauce

30 ml/2 tbsp cornflour (cornstarch)

Heat the oil, salt and garlic until the garlic turns light golden. Add the chicken and stir-fry for 2 minutes. Add the onions, water chestnuts and pineapple and stir-fry for 2 minutes. Add the wine or sherry, stock and sugar and season with pepper. Bring to the boil, cover and simmer for 5 minutes. Mix together the pineapple juice, soy sauce and cornflour. Stir into the pan and simmer, stirring until the sauce thickens and clears.

Chicken with Pineapple and Lychees

Serves 4

30 ml/2 tbsp groundnut (peanut) oil
225 g/8 oz chicken, thinly sliced
1 slice ginger root, minced
15 ml/1 tbsp soy sauce
15 ml/1 tbsp rice wine or dry sherry
200 g/7 oz canned pineapple chunks in syrup
200 g/7 oz canned lychees in syrup
15 ml/1 tbsp cornflour (cornstarch)

Heat the oil and fry the chicken until lightly coloured. Add the soy sauce and wine or sherry and stir well. Measure 250 ml/8 fl oz/1 cup of the mixed pineapple and lychee syrup and reserve 30 ml/2 tbsp. Add the rest to the pan, bring to the boil and simmer for a few minutes until the chicken is tender. Add the pineapple chunks and lychees. Mix the cornflour with the reserved syrup, stir into the pan and simmer, stirring, until the sauce clears and thickens.

Serves 4

1 chicken breast, thinly sliced

100 g/4 oz lean pork, thinly sliced

60 ml/4 tbsp soy sauce

15 ml/1 tbsp cornflour (cornstarch)

1 egg white

45 ml/3 tbsp groundnut (peanut) oil

3 slices ginger root, chopped

50 g/2 oz bamboo shoots, sliced

225 g/8 oz mushrooms, sliced

225 g/8 oz Chinese leaves, shredded

120 ml/4 fl oz/½ cup chicken stock

30 ml/2 tbsp water

Mix together the chicken and pork. Mix the soy sauce, 5 ml/1 tsp of cornflour and the egg white and stir into the chicken and pork. Leave to stand for 30 minutes. Heat half the oil and fry the chicken and pork until lightly browned then remove them from the pan. Heat the remaining oil and fry the ginger, bamboo shoots, mushrooms and Chinese leaves until well coated in oil. Add the stock and bring to the boil. Return the chicken mixture to the pan, cover and simmer for about 3 minutes until the meats are tender. Blend the remaining cornflour to a paste with the water, stir into the sauce and simmer, stirring, until the sauce thickens. Serve at once.

Braised Chicken with Potatoes

Serves 4

4 chicken pieces
45 ml/3 tbsp groundnut (peanut) oil
1 onion, sliced
1 clove garlic, crushed
2 slices ginger root, minced
450 ml/¾ pt/2 cups water
45 ml/3 tbsp soy sauce
15 ml/1 tbsp brown sugar
2 potatoes, cubed

Chop the chicken into 5 cm/2 in pieces. Heat the oil and fry the onion, garlic and ginger until lightly browned. Add the chicken and fry until lightly browned. Add the water and soy sauce and bring to the boil. Stir in the sugar, cover and simmer for about 30 minutes. Add the potatoes to the pan, cover and simmer for a further 10 minutes until the chicken is tender and the potatoes are cooked.

Five-Spice Chicken with Potatoes

Serves 4

45 ml/3 tbsp groundnut (peanut) oil

450 g/1 lb chicken, cut into chunks

salt

45 ml/3 tbsp yellow bean paste

45 ml/3 tbsp soy sauce

5 ml/1 tsp sugar

5 ml/1 tsp five-spice powder

1 potato, diced

450 ml/¾ pt/2 cups chicken stock

Heat the oil and stir-fry the chicken until lightly browned. Sprinkle with salt then stir in the bean paste, soy sauce, sugar and five-spice powder and stir-fry for 1 minute. Add the potato and stir in well then add the stock, bring to the boil, cover and simmer for about 30 minutes until tender.

Red-Cooked Chicken

Serves 4

450 g/1 lb chicken, sliced

120 ml/4 fl oz/½ cup soy sauce

15 ml/1 tbsp sugar

2 slices ginger root, finely chopped

90 ml/6 tbsp chicken stock

30 ml/2 tbsp rice wine or dry sherry

4 spring onions (scallions), sliced

Place all the ingredients in a pan and bring to the boil. Cover and simmer for about 15 minutes until the chicken is cooked through. Remove the lid and continue to simmer for about 5 minutes, stirring occasionally, until the sauce has thickened. Serve sprinkled with spring onions.

Chicken Rissoles

Serves 4

225 g/8 oz chicken meat, minced (ground)

3 water chestnuts, minced

1 spring onion (scallion), chopped

1 slice ginger root, minced

2 egg whites

5 ml/2 tsp salt

5 ml/1 tsp freshly ground pepper

120 ml/4 fl oz/½ cup groundnut (peanut) oil

5 ml/1 tsp chopped ham

Mix together the chicken, chestnuts, half the spring onion, the ginger, egg whites, salt and pepper. Shape into small balls and press flat. Heat the oil and fry the rissoles until golden brown, turning once. Serve sprinkled with the remaining spring onion and the ham.

Savoury Chicken

Serves 4

30 ml/2 tbsp groundnut (peanut) oil

4 chicken pieces

3 spring onions (scallions), chopped

2 cloves garlic, crushed

1 slice ginger root, chopped

120 ml/4 fl oz/½ cup soy sauce

30 ml/2 tbsp rice wine or dry sherry

30 ml/2 tbsp brown sugar

5 ml/1 tsp salt

375 ml/13 fl oz/1½ cups water

15 ml/1 tbsp cornflour (cornstarch)

Heat the oil and fry the chicken pieces until golden brown. Add the spring onions, garlic and ginger and fry for 2 minutes. Add the soy sauce, wine or sherry, sugar and salt and stir together well. Add the water and bring to the boil, cover and simmer for 40 minutes. Mix the cornflour with a little water, stir it into the sauce and simmer, stirring, until the sauce clears and thickens.

Chicken in Sesame Oil

Serves 4

90 ml/6 tbsp groundnut (peanut) oil

60 ml/4 tbsp sesame oil

5 slices ginger root

4 chicken pieces

600 ml/1 pt/2½ cups rice wine or dry sherry

5 ml/1 tsp sugar

salt and freshly ground pepper

Heat the oils and fry the ginger and chicken until lightly browned. Add the wine or sherry and season with sugar, salt and pepper. Bring to the boil and simmer gently, uncovered, until the chicken is tender and the sauce has reduced. Serve in bowls.

Sherry Chicken

Serves 4

30 ml/2 tbsp groundnut (peanut) oil

4 chicken pieces

120 ml/4 fl oz/½ cup soy sauce

500 ml/17 fl oz/2¼ cups rice wine or dry sherry

30 ml/2 tbsp sugar

5 ml/1 tsp salt

2 cloves garlic, crushed

1 slice ginger root, chopped

Heat the oil and fry the chicken until browned on all sides. Drain off excess oil and add all the remaining ingredients. Bring to the boil, cover and simmer over a fairly high heat for 25 minutes. Reduce the heat and simmer for a further 15 minutes until the chicken is cooked through and the sauce has reduced.

Chicken with Soy Sauce

Serves 4

350 g/12 oz chicken, diced

2 spring onions (scallions), chopped

3 slices ginger root, minced

15 ml/1 tbsp cornflour (cornstarch)

30 ml/2 tbsp rice wine or dry sherry

30 ml/2 tbsp water

45 ml/3 tbsp groundnut (peanut) oil

60 ml/4 tbsp thick soy sauce

5 ml/1 tsp sugar

Mix together the chicken, spring onions, ginger, cornflour, wine or sherry and water and leave to stand for 30 minutes, stirring occasionally. Heat the oil and stir-fry the chicken for about 3 minutes until lightly browned. Add the soy sauce and sugar and stir-fry for about 1 minute until the chicken is cooked through and tender.

Spicy Baked Chicken

Serves 4

150 ml/¼ pt/generous ½ cup soy sauce

2 cloves garlic, crushed

50 g/2 oz/¼ cup brown sugar

1 onion, finely chopped

30 ml/2 tbsp tomato purée (paste)

1 slice lemon, chopped

1 slice ginger root, minced

45 ml/3 tbsp rice wine or dry sherry

4 large chicken pieces

Mix together all the ingredients except the chicken. Place the chicken in an ovenproof dish, pour over the mixture, cover and marinate overnight, basting occasionally. Bake the chicken in a preheated oven at 180°C/350°F/gas mark 4 for 40 minutes, turning and basting occasionally. Remove the lid, raise the oven temperature to 200°C/400°F/gas mark 6 and continue to cook for a further 15 minutes until the chicken is cooked through.

Chicken with Spinach

Serves 4

100 g/4 oz chicken, minced

15 ml/1 tbsp ham fat, minced

175 ml/6 fl oz/¾ cup chicken stock

3 egg whites, lightly beaten

salt

5 ml/1 tsp water

450 g/1 lb spinach, finely chopped

5 ml/1 tsp cornflour (cornstarch)

45 ml/3 tbsp groundnut (peanut) oil

Mix together the chicken, ham fat, 150 ml/¼ pt/generous ½ cup of chicken stock, the egg whites, 5 ml/1 tsp of salt and the water. Mix the spinach with the remaining stock, a pinch of salt and the cornflour mixed with a little water. Heat half the oil, add the spinach mixture to the pan and stir constantly over a low heat until heated through. Transfer to a warmed serving plate and keep warm. Heat the remaining oil and fry spoonfuls of the chicken mixture until set and white. Arrange on top of the spinach and serve at once.

Serves 4

15 ml/1 tbsp groundnut (peanut) oil

pinch of salt

1 clove garlic, crushed

225 g/8 oz chicken, cut into strips

100 g/4 oz mushrooms, sliced

175 g/6 oz cabbage, shredded

100 g/4 oz bamboo shoots, shredded

50 g/2 oz water chestnuts, shredded

100 g/4 oz bean sprouts

5 ml/1 tsp sugar

5 ml/1 tsp rice wine or dry sherry

5 ml/1 tsp soy sauce

8 spring roll skins

oil for deep-frying

Heat the oil, salt and garlic and fry gently until the garlic begins to turn golden. Add the chicken and mushrooms and stir-fry for a few minutes until the chicken turns white. Add the cabbage, bamboo shoots, water chestnuts and bean sprouts and stir-fry for 3 minutes. Add the sugar, wine or sherry and soy sauce, stir well, cover and stir-fry for a final 2 minutes. Turn into a colander and leave to drain.

Place a few spoonfuls of the filling mixture in the centre of each spring roll skin, fold up the bottom, fold in the sides, then roll upwards, enclosing the filling. Seal the edge with a little flour and water mixture then leave to dry for 30 minutes. Heat the oil and deep-fry the spring rolls for about 10 minutes until crisp and golden brown. Drain well before serving.